The Story of the Southwold-Walberswick Ferry

Dedicated to the memory of
my father, David Church
(1942 – 2001)

The Story of the Southwold-Walberswick Ferry

By
Dani Church

with
Ann Gander

Published in 2009 by Dani Church

Design by Holm Oak Publishing
24 Church View, Holton, Halesworth, Suffolk IP19 8PB
Telephone: 01986 875999
www.holmoakpublishing.co.uk

Printed by Barnwell Print Ltd of Aylsham, Norfolk

ISBN 9780953340644

Also by Ann Gander:

Top Hats and Servants' Tales: A Century of Life on
Somerleyton Estate

Adrian Bell: Voice of the Countryside

Back cover photograph by Stephen Wolfenden

Contents

Acknowledgements

I should like to say a big thank you to all those who have contributed to this book by providing information, photos and memories. My thanks to Ann Gander, without whose enthusiasm, friendship and expertise this book would never have been completed, and to Crispin Chalker for all his encouragement and support throughout the whole of this project. All of my family have been a great help, especially my mum Julie, sister Polly and auntie, Hazel Church, who was always at the end of the phone when I needed to ask 'just one more question.'

I am indebted to everyone who is featured in this book for being a part of this amazing story, including Richard and Dorothy Fisk, Arthur Sharman, Mollie Robinson, Madge Beane, Chris Coleman, Vida Connick, Phillip Kett, Arthur and Gary Brown, and my thanks to all the families who shared their memories with me, including those of Ruby Canham, George Balls, Arthur Brown and Roger James, also to John English, Renee Waites, Dennis Long, Keith Rogers, Pam Hazelgrave and Richard Scott. For help with local history and family research my thanks to David Lee, Bernard Segrave-Daly, Michael Wickins, Christine Gilbert, the staff of Southwold Museum, Dunwich Museum and Lowestoft Record Office and members of the Walberswick Local History Society.

Grateful thanks also to Megan Jenkins of Country Life magazine for permission to quote from their letters page, to Sue Taylor for use of her interview with Young Bob, to Christopher Elliott for his anecdote and photos, also to Sir Charles Blois for permission to print the ferry licence from his family papers. Further thanks to Nolan Lincoln, picture editor at Archant for allowing me to reproduce pictures from their newspapers. Ian Collins of the Eastern Daily Press has been a big help, and my thanks to Times Newspapers and Simon Barnes for allowing me to print an extract of his very moving tribute to my dad, and also for writing the foreword. My gratitude to Anne Thornton who gave permission to use a number of photos by Frederick and A. Barrett Jenkins. Thank you to Paul Thompson for the wonderful poem, and to Bridget Cousins and Chris Coe for their lovely songs. Thanks also to James Hayward for invaluable advice.

Finally, my thanks to all the people who continue to support me in providing the ferry service, especially to Butch and Di Church, also to Crispin, Nick and Luke for working so hard on the oars.

Picture credits

I am truly grateful to all those people who have kindly loaned me their precious photographs, many of which have never been published before. In many cases we do not know who the photographer was, and I apologise for any omissions. In the case of the picture of George Todd on page 13, Ian Collins, author and journalist at the Eastern Daily Press, believes it may have been by P H Emerson. My thanks to Luke Jeans for extracting pictures from Arthur Brown's video of the boatbuilding work.

The credits are as follows; please excuse the brevity but may I say again a huge thank you to all the following for their kind permission to use their work, or any for which they hold the copyright.

Mark Harrison
Times Newspapers Ltd – Foreword page
Walberswick Local History Society
Southwold Museum
Stephen Wolfenden p35, p120, p136

Richard Johnston Bryden © p123,139
Lowestoft Record Office
Archant Newspapers
Ian Collins
Lord Nelson Inn
Tony Mathews p101
Lee Southgate p113
Christopher Elliott
Family of Frederick and A. Barrett Jenkins
Christine Gilbert
Pam Hardy
Hazel Church
Chris Coleman
Harry Edwards
Alice and Andrew Eastaugh
Julie Church
Michael Bullen p144, p162, p195
Keith Rogers
Marion Welton
Richard Fisk
Frank Reed
Vida Connick
Ron Hall
Pam Hazelgrave
Peter and Antonia Hunt
Family of Ruby Canham
Mollie Robinson
Family of Arthur Brown
Family of John Robert James
Luke Jeans

Foreword

The ferry plies between Southwold and Walberswick, but that's not all it does. It also plies between the present and the past. Every five-minute crossing is a journey through time.

Even on our holidays we are pursued by the furies of time. We have to make the pub before they stop serving food, we find ourselves driving fast along the main roads just because it is our habit, modern communications make sure that the world we live in is always with us, picking up emails or taking phone-calls in the tea-shop and the sea-front.

But then we walk from Southwold towards Walberswick and the river brings us up short. At once we slip into timelessness, into continuity, into a different pace of being, a different way of thinking. You have to go at the river's pace. There is no other option.

The tourist must make contact with a person doing one of the oldest jobs in civilisation. The river-crossing is made at a place where people have crossed the river for centuries. The unhurried nature of the journey links every passenger with all those who have crossed before. The ferry is part of a continuum: ferries have linked and separated the two communities of Southwold and Walberswick for centuries. What's more, the person doing the rowing has links with a trade that has been passed down the family for generations.

The ferry is efficient all right, but this is not efficiency as we know it. It is not about straight lines and high technology: it is about the economy of effort, the way the rowers use the river and their knowledge. Each crossing would be a battle for a novice, rendering him a wreck after a dozen crossings: the rowers of the ferry make it a form of judo, in which they use the strength of the river to their own advantage, conning the reluctant river into cooperation.

Every ferry-crossing is a small gift of calm. Between engine and engine, between deadline and deadline, between phone-call and phone-call, between one appointment and the next, there is the ferry. It is neither one thing nor the other, neither Southwold nor Walberswick, neither past nor present: but for many visitors it is the hidden high spot of their time in Suffolk.

Oh, the times gone were hard, the people who lived in them were poor in ways we simply can't understand, and they suffered in ways unthinkable to us. But every advance comes at a price: and we have lost the feeling that nature dictates the pace of our lives. We are no longer in the habit of letting rivers set the agenda.

But once you stand on the jetty, the river – nature – takes over. The wait for the boat, the arc of the crossing – a journey that covers almost three times the width of the river when the water is at its quickest – and you are savouring something all holiday-makers seek: a break from the 21st century, a trip to a time when time had another value.

I crossed the river time and again with David Church, and our families became friends. Daisy, who served her time as ferry dog, was born in my house, to my Labrador bitch. I cheered when Dani Church gained her qualifications, and I was one of her first legal passengers. The ferry is part of my history: but then it becomes part of everybody's history. That is what it is for. Getting from A to B, or rather from S to W, is very much a secondary matter.

Dani has done a marvellous job here of putting together the history of the ferry and the legion of people – good people, kind people, rum buggers and all -- who have propelled it. Dani has handled her material with the same insouciance with which she controls the big hardwood boat and its load of passengers – "hands inside the boat, please" -- when the River Blyth is at its stroppiest. As usual, the trickiest passages are handled with the greatest aplomb. The ferry is one of Suffolk's small gifts to its visitors: with this book, you have the ferry with you always.

Simon Barnes

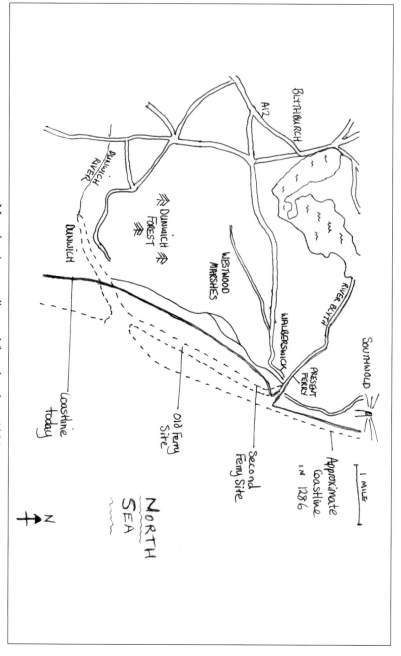

Map showing coastline and ferry locations, 1286

Introduction

Years ago, my dad David Church, who was then ferryman, said he thought it might be a good idea to produce a booklet giving a brief history of the ferry. Sadly, he didn't manage to bring his idea to fruition, but over the past four years I have been researching and collecting information and photographs, and this book is the result. It has turned out to be much more than the 'booklet' Dad had in mind – largely due to the enormous help and encouragement I've received along the way, and all of the wonderful stories that simply had to be included.

Although the book is basically about the history of the Southwold – Walberswick Ferry, I have included all that is known about the men and women who have worked the route over the centuries. Sometimes their term of employment overlapped, so it has not been possible to keep it in strictly chronological order. I felt that every one of them deserved their 'voice;' as through changing times and seasons they have kept on travelling back and forth across the River Blyth. They must have seen so many events and been such a part of the community, that their small but significant contribution to the lives of the people in the surrounding towns and villages should not be overlooked.

For those readers who are not so familiar with the region, it may be helpful to consider the layout of the land. There is widespread discussion nowadays about weather patterns and their effect on coastal regions, but in this part of East Anglia, around the mouth of the River Blyth, residents learned long ago that Nature will have its way. As wind and sea did battle with the shore, the inhabitants of Dunwich, Southwold and Walberswick simply had to make the best of what they had.

It is well known in these parts that Dunwich was once a major town and port with thousands of inhabitants, but from the thirteenth century onwards much of it was lost to the sea, giving it the title 'East Anglia's Atlantis.' In what's left of the village, a small museum exhibits artifacts from the past and contains a model of the once mighty town. With romantic ruins of the old priory, a few cottages and a wonderful fish and chip restaurant, Dunwich is now a small but worthwhile dot on the tourist map.

Next along the coast, Walberswick, now a charming hamlet with fishermen's cottages and a few shops, was once a thriving trading post with Europe. This picturesque village, long a favourite haunt of artists, has had its share of drama, with evidence of smuggling, rebellion, and the destruction of much of its church by Dowsing's men and others. Today the villagers' major concern is the stealthily rising sea, as well as rocketing house prices.

North of here lies Southwold, a fashionable resort in old-fashioned terms, with eccentric amusements on the refurbished pier and a fine lighthouse. Its proud heritage includes the Adnams brewery, and six enormous cannons facing out to sea, which may have originally been intended for sinking invaders.

There has long been friendly (and not so friendly) rivalry between the three neighbours, but all the while sturdy men, and sometimes women, were ferrying passengers, goods and even animals back and forth across the river, rowing rhythmically or, during a period of mechanisation, conducting the chain-ferry on its way, quietly, without fuss, and with skill and, mostly, good cheer.

That tradition, started over 750 years ago still goes on today. I am proud that my family has had a long association with the ferry, going back five generations and more than 120 years. I've included an extract of our family tree to show which of the ferrymen were relations of mine, but this book is also a tribute to the other men and women who came to work this invaluable route.

Dani Church   March 2009

Extract of CROSS / CHURCH FAMILY TREE
Ferrymen shown in bold

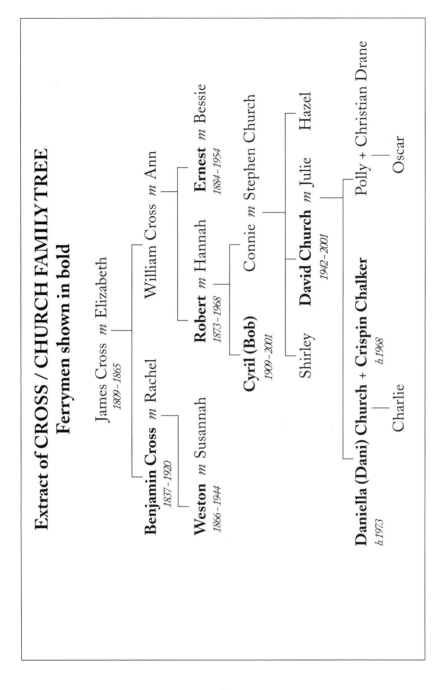

James Cross *m* Elizabeth
1809–1865

William Cross *m* Ann

Benjamin Cross *m* Rachel
1837–1920

Robert *m* Hannah
1873–1968

Ernest *m* Bessie
1884–1954

Weston *m* Susannah
1866–1944

Cyril (Bob)
1909–2001

Connie *m* Stephen Church

Shirley

David Church *m* Julie
1942–2001

Hazel

Polly + Christian Drane

Daniella (Dani) Church + **Crispin Chalker**
b.1973   *b.1968*

Charlie

Oscar

Ferry licence dated 1559

Chapter one

The Shifting Sands of Fortune

The first recorded mention of a ferry in this area was during an Inquisition at Dunwich in 1236. It shows that Lady Margery de Cressy, a local heiress whose two successive husbands actually held the title and power, argued that, as there was a right for the Burgesses of Dunwich to have a ferry boat operating from their side of the river, charging one halfpenny per man and horse, so should there be another on Lady de Cressy's side, paying her a similar amount. This was agreed.

On the opposite side, the ferry was licensed to Sir Roger Swillington, or rather it was written that he 'farmed' the ferry boat of the Burgesses of Dunwich at the annual rent of 20 shillings. Clearly he would not have been doing the rowing himself and sadly there is no record of who the actual ferryman was. There is no mention either of how the two businesses shared or divided the custom – whether each could only take passengers from their side to the other and must return empty, or whether they could ply their trade in both directions.

However they managed it, one has to marvel at their skill; how tricky it must have been to row a man and his horse across the river, if the animal was in any way flighty or nervous. Just persuading it to board the boat would have been a feat. According to some stories, a much larger creature – an elephant - would one day be taken on board the ferry.

In Medieval times the River Blyth did not flow into the sea at Southwold as it does today; instead it meandered three miles along the coast south from Southwold before it flowed out to sea at Dunwich Port. These ferries were needed to cross the port, so the site of the original ferry was towards Dunwich at the Old Haven. It seems there was also a road bridge across the river at this time, but little more is known about it.

In 1328 a hurricane-force wind and storm surge caused a massive shift of the shingle spit at Dunwich, which stoppered up the harbour entrance. Visiting ships began taking their business to Walberswick, causing bitter arguments to break out between the inhabitants of the two towns, and a number of deaths are said to have occurred.

Towards the end of the 15th century Dunwich was stripped of its status as a Haven Port and the King granted a Royal Charter, bestowing the title on Southwold Harbour. It was a bitter blow for the people of Dunwich, as if they hadn't suffered enough already.

Meanwhile the ferries continued and a rare copy of a licence agreement can be found in the papers of the Blois family, who have been major landowners in the area for centuries. Dated 1559, it grants Robert Bardewell, a merchant from Walberswick, the lease of two ferries and ferryboats for a period of 21 years. The ferries were to be operated between Walberswick and Dunwich, and from Walberswick to Southwold.

Having the ferry rights was one thing; being able to operate them was another. Clogging of the waterway continued to be an issue and not long after that time, in 1590, a new cut – effectively a short cut - was opened, close to its present position.

Disputes over land holdings and rights to fees, ships' dues and taxes continued, and records in the National Archives at Kew, Surrey, show that between 1590 and 1592 actions were taken by the bailiffs of Dunwich who accused landowners and residents of Southwold and Walberswick of stopping up the mouth of the harbour. In turn the people of Walberswick were reported as refusing to pay the yearly rent of 20 shillings due to the town of Dunwich for 'the farm of a ferry.'

Another record for the time shows that Sir Arthur Hopton,

lord of the manor of Blythburgh, was claiming jurisdiction over the river between there and Walberswick, and that the mouth of the haven was 'not within the liberties of Dunwich' – therefore he was also said to own the ferries and rights.

While all of this wrangling was going on, the ferrymen would simply have carried on doing their job for as long as they were employed by whoever held the rights at the time. Dunwich, already described as a decaying town, was losing out all round and even as it was being forced to surrender land to neighbouring lords, ever more of its coastline was disappearing into the sea.

It does appear that a boat service continued in the vicinity, for in 1616 a tragic accident occurred there. The Parish Register for Southwold states:

'The names of those that have drowned and fonde again: they were drowned in our haven comeing from Dunwich fayer on St James daye in a bote by reason of one cable laying over warf the haven for by reason the men that brought them downe was so negligent that when they were redie to come ashore the bote broke lose and so the force of the tide carried the bote against the cable and so overwhelmed. The number of them were xxii but they were not all found.

The Widow Robson

John Bootes

Marye Yewell

Suzan Frost

Margarett Blackbourne and the Widow Langley were all buried upon the 20 daie of Julye being all caste away coming from Dunwich fayer on St James day.

Widow Foster was buried the 27 daie of Julye.

Bennet Allen was buried the 30 daie.

Goodie Kensum was buried the same daie.

Mrs Ward and Elizabeth Yonges, daughter to Mr Yonges, vicar and minister, was buried the 31 daie of Julye.

All these were founde again in this towne and buried.'

The following picture is part of an old illustration depicting a hand-cranked chain ferry at Walberswick, and may be of the kind that sank on that tragic night.

By 1618 there were calls by the people of the three towns for government help to keep the haven open, and in the Trinity House of Deptford Transactions it was noted that failure to act would mean that the haven would become 'darved up' and irrecoverable, to the ruin of the inhabitants and to the prejudice of the shipping and seamen of the kingdom.

In 1633 there was trouble of a man-made kind when landowner Sir John Rowse created two sluices on his part of the river, blocking the channel and preventing access for the fishermen of Dunwich, Southwold and Walberswick. The complainants took their case to the Admiralty court, and it appears that they won, although not until some time later the next year.

So the waterway stayed open, and with it, the ferry service. Two documents in the Blois Estate archives refer to the 'apprizement' of ferry boats in 1641 and 1671. Meanwhile in 1659 a huge fire swept through Southwold, destroying most of the public buildings and 238 houses, causing much of the population to flee to the neighbouring villages. One can imagine the ferrymen helping to carry terrified people and their possessions away from the inferno.

In the latter part of this century the North Sea would become the meeting-place for the warring English and Dutch fleets, and in the second of these, The Battle of Lowestoft fought in June 1665, more than 200 ships took part. The noise must have made the earth shudder, and caused terror for the inhabitants of the coastal towns.

The Dutch suffered their worst ever naval defeat, but still they returned to fight once more. The Battle of Sole Bay took place off the coast of Southwold on the 26th May 1672, and it must have been a spectacular but dreadful sight for those on the land as English mariners took on the Dutch fleet in another struggle that resulted in the deaths of many men, including the Earl of Sandwich. It has been recorded that bodies were washed up for many days after, and over 800 wounded from both sides were landed at Southwold. One imagines that the ferrymen would surely have taken part in the rescue missions.

An early illustration showing the view from Walberswick,
looking across the River Blyth to Southwold

By 1746 the harbour had again become silted and choked, and an act of parliament, the Southwold Harbour Act, demanded that it should be cleared. The control of the harbour was passed to 22 commissioners who were able to raise money to build timber piers at the harbour mouth and reduce the silting and scouring action of the incoming sea. The piers soon took a battering and had to be strengthened. In 1757 the River Blyth Navigation Act went further in insisting that the river be made navigable to Halesworth, a small town nine miles inland, and for a time there was renewed prosperity in the region. Local author Rachel Lawrence gives much detail about these events in her excellent book *Southwold River*.

Records show that the powerful Blois family was making good use of their entitlement to sea wrecks and groundage of all ships and goods that might be cast up on the shore in their manor, and in addition they were taking advantage of their manorial right to the quay at Walberswick, which allowed them to charge wharfage rents. These amounts were small and difficult to collect so the family leased the rights to others at around £21 a year. By 1772 one Richard Burchett is shown paying £24 a year for the wharfage rights and also the rent of the ferry. It is assumed that Burchett employed a ferryman to do the hard labour of rowing, but sadly his identity is unknown.

At this time the quay at Walberswick was kept busy with shiploads of grain, cheeses, butter and other farm produce being sent to London and Rotterdam, while timber, coal, chalk, brandy and other spirits were being brought back in.

Still the elements of Nature continued to defy the people of the three coastal towns, and still the people stood firm, holding regular meetings to discuss the navigation and consider new ways to deal with the creeping sand and silt. By the late 18th century landowners were seeking to drain the marshes more efficiently, erecting a mill to pump the water, and channelling it into the river via a sluice at Walberswick. Even this 'blew up' in 1779 necessitating the construction of a new sluice and cut plus yet more repairs to walls and the wharf itself.

There were problems at Southwold too, with shifting shingle choking the harbour so that in 1810 and 1811 the entrance had to be dug out no less that six times. Following winter gales, by February 1827 it was blocked again, and at least once more by 1839.

The conflict was not all Man against Nature: long after the naval battles at sea, small skirmishes took place in the rivers as smugglers tested the mettle of customs officers and risked their lives to bring contraband ashore. In 1750 the situation was so bad that the government sent a detachment of Dragoons to nearby Blythburgh to try to bring order to the region. Sadly one of their number, a black drummer named Toby Gill, was found drunk and insensible next to the body of a Walberswick girl one morning. He was hanged for her murder, although there is much doubt about his guilt, and his name lives on in a local place name, in legend and in many a ghost story.

It is said that the smugglers themselves latched on to any spooky tale that might help dissuade people from wandering about at night and possibly disturbing their activities. Some say that the famous 'Black Shuck' devil dog legend is simply another one of these tall tales put about to keep people locked up in their homes at night while the contraband men were about their work. In 1821 the smugglers managed to land up to 400 tubs of liquor at Reydon quay, and by the time customs officials arrived the men and their booty were long gone, leaving their boat abandoned on Blythburgh flats.

On a lighter note, local businessman and diarist James Maggs wrote in October 1832 that a wager had taken place between John Cottingham and Robert Bird when the former bet the latter that he couldn't walk from Southwold to Dunwich in an hour and a half or less. Bird did it in forty seven and a half minutes, winning the bet – a seemingly impossible feat because the only way across the river was by ferry. However, the crafty man had arranged for a number of boats to be placed across so that he could step from one to another and 'walk' across. No doubt the ferryman was bemused by the sight and although he had missed out on a fare, he would have known that such a prank was unlikely to be repeated.

Maggs also kept news cuttings, one of which shows that in December 1862 a severe gale at Southwold had swept away everything standing on the beach, including fishermen's huts, boat houses and boats. Again in 1864 the elements took their toll: the sea made such inroads that it claimed the coast guard watch-house, the path from New York Cliff to Gun Hill and a portion of Miss Hudson's garden.

In Maggs's time the sea and river are shown to be places of danger time and again, with notes about wrecks and drownings commonplace. During all this time the ferrymen, although not immune to the battles being waged out at sea and in the closer confines of the harbour and its river, nevertheless carried on rowing to and fro, steadily passing on their way. They must have seen many a strange goings-on, whether mortal or other-worldly, but for the most part their stories have died with them.

Chapter two

George Todd: 'I knows it'

George Todd is probably the most famous ferryman of them all, renowned for his dry sense of humour and razor-sharp wit. He had many succinct sayings, and when anyone tried to impart any ferryside news or gossip he would nod and reply, 'I knows it'. In time this became even briefer, until eventually if a passenger observed that it was a fine morning Todd would say 'I know't.'

Todd – photographer unknown but possibly P.H. Emerson

Born in Walberswick in 1808 George went out to work as an agricultural labourer at an early age and in about 1835 he married a local girl named Elizabeth. He was soon fathering children at the usual average rate of one every other year. In total the couple had ten children and most lived to adulthood, which in itself was quite an achievement for those times. In some ways the growing family was close-knit, for when the sibling Todds found spouses of their own and began to produce the next generation, they would help each other with child-minding and support. There appear to have been two illegitimate offspring, who went to live with their grandparents George and Elizabeth, and one branch of the family moved north to Durham.

Of several Todd children there is no trace as to their fate, but in a book written by Ernest Cooper and published in 1932, he included an anecdote about one son, nicknamed Harry, who said that he had once gone to sea for twelve years without even writing a letter home, but then turned up 'out of the blue', much to his father's disbelief. It is unclear who 'Harry' was, but it is most likely that this was George junior, who failed to find much work as a fisherman and went to sea with his brother Charles in the 1880s. 'Harry' himself fathered ten children and lived out his days in Southwold.

George Todd senior was all set to continue his work as a farmhand, but at some point in the 1850s when he was already middle-aged, he agreed to step in for another man who plied the ferry. George managed the job well and awaited the return of the regular ferryman, but he never came back. What had been intended as a favour for a few days became George's new career, and he carried on ferrying for another thirty years.

In his early rowing days Todd used to work the 'hoss' boat across the river. This boat was long enough to convey a horse or even a trap, although probably not both at the same time, so presumably a double journey and fee would have been required. Later a much smaller rowing boat was used.

Todd is described as a most picturesque character with sharp, twinkly blue eyes and a full, tangled beard not dissimilar to a bird's nest; he often wore a battered Spanish-style straw hat. Described as having a large frame, he held himself erect and it was said that whatever the weather, his strong arms would be ready for service.

Numerous fanciful writers have said that he bore a strong resemblance to Charon, the famous Styx ferryman in Greek

Mythology, but Todd mostly carried only the living. However, an area so steeped in turbulent history is bound to have its ghost stories, and in the book *The Story of Southwold*, edited by Janet Becker and published in 1948, Janet relates the eerie experience of a passenger on the Walberswick ferry many years earlier.

As the man walked down to the shore he overtook an old man leading a child by the hand. Assuming they were fellow passengers he told Todd to wait for them, but when he looked back he saw that the road was empty. George simply said 'We never waits for *them.*'

On another occasion a lady tried to enquire about his religious interests. When asked if he went to church Todd, droll as ever, replied, 'Well, no marm, I can't exactly say as how I do. But then I rows across many as does.'

That anecdote was published in a letter which appeared in the *Ipswich Journal* of January 1885. The writer went on in his reminiscing about Old Todd, 'A peculiar trait in the old man's character was a special and deeply-rooted dislike of persons who stood up in his boat. To a shop boy once who persisted in the obnoxious practice Todd severely remarked, "I have heered a deal of talk lately about shop assistants sittin' down."'

Todd's manner of expression was, as the writer said 'Native all over' and left his passengers in no doubt as to his views and preferences. Another time, when the crossing was wet and the wind was blowing hard a passenger stood up to avoid sitting on the wet seat. As progress across the river was slow he dared to remark that they were taking a long time getting over and Todd gruffly retorted, 'Yes and if you don't sit down it'll be a hell of a time.'

It could be said that old George didn't suffer fools, he could be blunt and even surly, and also it seems that he was not one for idle chit-chat. Apparently when he one day appeared in a brand new pair of boots, some saw this as quite an event, for boots could often be made to last a lifetime. A cheerful passenger ventured to remark, 'Why Mr Todd, you've a new pair of boots on today,' which brought the sardonic reply, 'I know. I put 'em there.'

Jot of ferrymen at Walker sand

16

Todd's fame spread far and wide, for he was captured both in oils and in rhyme. In 1880 the satirical magazine *Punch* published a poem entitled *A Warble of Walberswick* in which the second stanza states:

There's a harbour old and rotten, planks and anchors long forgotten
'Mid the tangle of the cordage: boats whose sea career is o'er;
There's a ferry with scant traffic, which McCullum and the Graphic
Sketched long years ago, and sea-gulls sweep along the lonesome shore

In another *Punch* poem, this one entitled *Artist on the Brain*, it says,

They sketch the ferryman's old hut, the reeds that sway and nod,
The early Christian countenance of Charon, Mister Todd.

Todd's hut, c.1881

George Todd did appear in many paintings, one of the most famous being the one shown above, which is by Frank E Cox. The original is lost but a copy hangs in the Lord Nelson Inn in Southwold, attracting much interest. In the picture Todd is seen helping an elderly lady into his boat with great care. However it appears that George must have at least partially retired by 1882, when the artist Henry Garland came to Walberswick and captured the ferryman at work – in this case it is recorded that the man at the oars is Todd's successor Benjamin Cross.

It is known that Todd was often assisted by Robert English, a Walberswick fisherman of the same age. The two men are captured in the photo on the following page, both of them wearing their trademark hats and Todd has his much-loved neckerchief knotted at his throat. The snap was probably taken in the late 1870s, the photographer is unknown.

Todd was an outstanding man, but he was never a wealthy one. His wife Elizabeth died in 1884 and in the following year the correspondent to the *Ipswich Journal* noted that 'poor old Todd', now in his late seventies, had fallen on hard times. He had, said the writer, been 'laid by, like one of the pink and blue hulks that surround his cabin. The parish allows him one shilling a week and half a stone of flour. His wages were never grand. Pension he has none.'

A plea is then made for twenty pounds to be raised in order to save Todd from ending his days in the workhouse, and the letter ends on a happy note, saying that some money was already 'to hand.'

Fortunately George Todd did not have to suffer the misery of an old age spent in the Bulcamp workhouse. The census for 1891 shows him living with his married daughter Hannah Jackson, and his status of 'Living on Own Means' suggests that he did have a little money from well-wishers to help him pay his way. George died at the age of 83 on the 18th of November that year.

George Todd (left) with Robert English

Memories of Todd continue to be handed down, and back in 1929, almost forty years after his death, a London resident named Mr T. Kelly wrote a letter to *The Times*, reminiscing about Southwold and one man in particular. Mr Kelly said he had played a boyish prank on the ferryman by dropping his rowlock overboard, and had had to pay a shilling out of his pocket-money in compensation.

He went on, 'I think he must have gone to bed with a pipe in his mouth. He made quite an income from the summer artists, who loved his rugged face set off with a scarlet neckerchief and blue jersey. Todd 'didn't hold' with the Southwold Railway, and when it approached the swing bridge above Walberswick, increasing to a roar as it passed over the 'jam pot,' he would shake his head and say 'them fules' would find themselves in the mud one of these days.'

No doubt if such an event had ever happened, on hearing the news Todd would surely have nodded sagely and declared 'I knows it.'

George Todd at the door of his hut

Chapter three

The River Blyth Ferry Company

The railway arrived in 1879, linking Southwold to Walberswick, Blythburgh, Wenhaston, Halesworth and beyond. It crossed the River Blyth on a 146 foot (44.5 metre) swing bridge, which in theory was not accessible to pedestrians, although there are stories of brave or foolhardy people taking a chance and jumping across the sleepers, usually if they had missed the last ferry.

Todd couldn't have seen the train crossing the bridge from his position down on the river, but he certainly would have heard it loudly enough, and observed its whorls of smoke and steam. The old man may have simply disliked change but he had good cause for concern, because no sooner had the local people secured the basic line, then they were talking about expansion including a line to the harbour. Then they began asking for a new bridge: one that would threaten Todd's livelihood.

In September 1881 the Earl of Stradbroke, chairing a meeting of the Harbour Commissioners, suggested that the local transport system needed a vehicular bridge across the river at Walberswick. This was agreed in principle, but the cost was deemed to be prohibitive; the bridge itself would cost up to £1,500 but there would be an additional £600-£700 needed to pass the necessary Act of Parliament. Nevertheless Stradbroke urged his fellow members to see if they could drum up subscriptions. The scheme made no discernable progress.

Apparently it was then decided that a more robust ferry than Todd's rowing boat would be the next best option, and in May 1884 the clerk of Southwold Town Council wrote to Sir John Blois, asking him to sell his rights in the Walberswick Ferry. However, Squire Blois had already been in legal wranglings with the railway company for compensation over lost land, and he was in no mood to acquiesce.

The Town Council tried again in November, this time asking Blois to provide a horse ferry within six months. They resolved that if he didn't comply, they would re-think the problem and produce a report.

Sir John remained steadfast and his letter of reply was published in the *Ipswich Journal*, in which he said that it was unreasonable to expect him to incur costs of £400 to put in a horse ferry when the Council might then build a bridge and take away all the trade. Alternatively, he could foresee the expensive boat being swept away due to the imminent collapse of the near-derelict harbour piers.

Now the heavy hand of local enterprise took up the case. In the same edition of the newspaper there was a letter stating, 'If Sir John is afraid to carry out his promise of putting a ferry-boat down for horses and carriages, I am quite willing to subscribe towards the cost of doing so, and I have no doubt the money required can be easily raised in the district...' This weighty gauntlet was thrown down by none other than Arthur C. Pain, engineer and manager of the Southwold Railway.

Pain was not a local man: he worked as a consultant engineer with an office in London, and he had been travelling the country devising, promoting and building light railway schemes with great enthusiasm. If he had one short-coming, it was that on occasion he would be proved to have underestimated costs, but here in Southwold he could call upon some wealthy and influential partners.

Henry Johnson Debney, a Southwold businessman with a shop at South Green, banded together with Ernest Adnams who had acquired the Sole Bay Brewery, and together they applied to Blois for the right of ferriage across the river.

It is worth pausing to consider the characters involved in this new scheme, and thanks to the research of former Managing Director of Adnams and Company Limited, Mr Bernard Segrave-Daly, a clear picture emerges. He says, 'Ernest Adnams was a keen huntsman and rode with the Waveney Harriers. He was a great admirer of Randolph Churchill and he was also a thrifty man; he knew a good investment when he saw one!'

Bernard has also looked at the business pedigree of Henry John Debney, finding that he had 'fingers in many pies.'

Sole Bay Brewery, about 1872

Debney had been manager of the Southwold Fishing Company but progressed to being a 'family grocer, tea dealer, wine merchant, woollen draper and house agent.' By 1883 he had moved upmarket as a 'licensed valuer and also a dealer in antique furniture and picture dealer,' and soon added Agent for Sun, Fire and Accident Insurance Co and Bank Manager for Gurneys to his list of titles. His firm had a large front-page advert in the *Halesworth Times* each week.

So these two men were big names in local business, and they were able to persuade Sir John Blois to let them have the ferry rights for an initial term of thirty years. That was quite a bold move, and the agreement was signed on 16ᵗʰ July 1885.

Immediately the men arranged to sub-let the lease to the newly formed River Blyth Ferry Company. True to Arthur Pain's word, he had managed to persuade enough people to put up the £500 needed to install the new ferry. The first directors were Justice of the Peace Colonel Heneage Charles Bagot-Chester, who was also chairman of the Southwold Railway Company, Arthur Cadlick Pain himself, and Adnams's brewing partner Thomas Sergeant. As for the latter, Bernard Segrave Daly says, 'Sergeant was a brewer brought in to partnership to provide additional finance to help Ernest Adnams develop the brewing business of the Sole Bay Brewery.' It seems that although Sergeant also became a shareholder of the River Blyth Ferry Company, this was not seen as his personal investment, but a holding of the firm Adnams and Sergeant.

With the finance in place it was simply a matter of installing the equipment. Good news was forthcoming in an article in the *Halesworth Times* dated 15ᵗʰ September 1885. It announced, 'In that wise spirit of compromise by which so many difficulties in the political and social world are solved, the inhabitants of Southwold, after heroic but fruitless attempts to obtain a bridge over the Blyth, are about to substitute a pontoon ferry for the present slow and imperfect means of transit.'

In similarly lyrical tones it added, 'At an expense of a little under £400 an excellent and not uncomely apparatus will be in its place at Michaelmas, well fenced in at the sides and ends, worked upon chains capable of carrying over with safety and comfort a van and a pair of horses with 8 tons of merchandise and 30 passengers if such a demand is requisite.'

This was indeed much more than Todd had ever been able to carry in his rowing boat, and yet it was said that the 'fare for foot passengers will not exceed the charge heretofore made.'

In fact the River Blyth Ferry Company came into existence proper when it was registered on the 28th September 1885 with solicitor Walter C Tuck as Secretary, but there were still a few snags to overcome before the new and much-vaunted service was up and running. On 2nd February 1886 it was reported that the new pontoon ferry had been delayed by 'difficulties with regard to the dock and landing stage on the Walberswick side.' By mid June, however, the ferry was in action. The local newspaper declared, 'No difficulty whatever is experienced in conveying carriages or waggons, and it is worked with the greatest ease and with much expedition. The traffic increases weekly...'

It is interesting that the journalist cheerfully describes the working of the ferry as being easy – the original pontoon was hauled across on chains by means of a hand-cranked wheel and one imagines it was anything but easy. In the first nine months the ferry carried 33,680 foot passengers, 723 drivers and vehicles, 69 extra horses and 403 'persons and trucks.' The income would have been around £300.

Still there were more difficulties to overcome: continual silting of the harbour and river meant that the pontoon was prone to grounding. As if to prove a point, in January 1887 Mr Charles Balls was reported to have driven a horse and cart across the river bed without need of the ferry at all. Amid much consternation the ferry company assured potential customers that it was only during exceptionally low tides that the ferry might experience problems. However in January 1891 during a severe winter, the River Blyth was frozen over almost to the harbour mouth and the ferry had to be suspended for two days. Meanwhile many locals found another way across – on skates.

The hand-cranked pontoon ferry

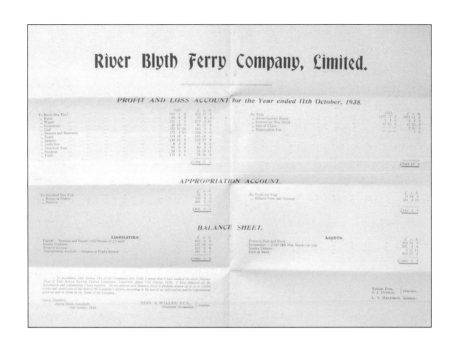

Accounts of the River Blyth Ferry Company

There was another suspension of ferry crossings in January 1895 following an exceptionally high and violent tide that caused a great deal of damage along the river. However, the ferry continued to make money. In November 1897 the *Halesworth Times* reported a good year-end profit for the company which, it said, 'is an eminently successful result for an enterprise that was viewed with very little favour when it was first entered upon.' This comment reflects the mixed feelings that had been prevalent when the new scheme was announced, but for the time being, the enterprise was turning out to be a great success.

According to local historian David Lee, financial returns from the operation in 1896 paid a dividend of 10% for investors, while in 1898 this increased to 15%. In 1905 it was a very welcome 20%.

By 1899 the service was in such demand that a steam-driven engine was fitted to the pontoon at a cost of £111. A newspaper report dated 18th July stated, 'The Ferry Company have found it necessary, owing to the constant increase of traffic, to fit up the Pontoon with steam power. Messrs Elliott and Garrod, Engineers of Beccles, were entrusted with the job and traffic was resumed under the new conditions on Monday morning. The engine takes up very little room, and the noise is no more than from the old arrangement of cog-wheels and crank. In default of a bridge, no better means of transit can exist than that now provided.'

Things were now going well for the ferryman too; not only had his job become easier, but in the early days he was paid an annual bonus of two guineas – £2.10 in today's money but a nice little extra when his wage was less than £80 a year. He might have enjoyed an elevated job title too – in some areas the operator on a chain-ferry pontoon was called a Floating Bridge Conductor.

However, the aesthetic value of the ferry had all but gone, and along with it went the artists and the poets. Todd's successor would not be captured in oils, rhyme or memoirs, but we do know that Benjamin Cross took up the role in the early days and started a dynasty that would continue to the present day.

The River Blyth Ferry Company, Limited.

TABLE OF TOLLS

EACH WAY.

The Ferryman is instructed to collect the Tolls at each journey.

For Each Person on foot from 2 years old upwards - - ½d.

„ Horse, Donkey, or Mule with a Vehicle and Driver, and each Motor Car and Driver - - 3d.

„ additional Horse, Donkey, or Mule with a Vehicle 2d.

„ Person in addition to the Driver in a Vehicle - ½d.

„ Bicycle, Tricycle, Bath Chair, Perambulator, Wheelbarrow, or Hand Truck, and Person in charge thereof - - - - - - - 1½d.

„ Motor Bicycle or Tricycle and person in charge thereof - - - - - - - - 2d.

„ Trailer - - - - - - - - 1d.

„ Horse, Donkey, or Mule, not drawing any Vehicle and each head of Cattle - - - .. - 2d.

„ Person mounted on or in charge thereof - - ½d.

„ Dog - - - - - - - - - ½d.

For Each **Sheep, Lamb, Goat, Pig** or other animal not hereinbefore mentioned up to ten in number - **1d.**

  „   **Sheep, Lamb, Goat,** or **Pig,** exceeding ten in number - - - - - - - - **½d.**

  „   **Goat and Carriage and Person in charge** - - **2d.**

GOODS, WARES, AND MERCHANDISE.

  „   **Parcel or Package, exceeding 56 lbs. in weight** and not being loaded in any Vehicle - - **1d.** per Cwt. or Fraction of One Cwt.

  „   **Ton of Cargo loaded or unloaded at the Company's Wharf** - - - - - - **2d.** (Demurrage after 3 days must be arranged and paid for as an extra charge)

  „   **Vessel mooring at the Company's Wharf** - - **2s.**

N.B.—*The Company reserve to themselves the right by their Servants, or Agents, to refuse to carry any traffic which in their opinion would involve extra risk, by reason of its being of a Dangerous or exceptional Character, or otherwise.*

N.B.—The Company also reserve to themselves the right from time to time to modify or vary this Table of Tolls in such manner as they may think proper.

N.B.—The Landing Stage is the Property of the Company and may not be used for other Boats except by permission.

HOURS OF TRAFFIC.

	WEEK DAYS.		SUNDAYS.	
	From a.m.	To p.m.	From a.m.	To p.m.
From the 6th day of April to the 11th day of October	6 0	9 0	7 0	9 0
From the 11th day of October to the 6th day of April	7 0	8 0	7 0	8 0

THE PONTOON SERVICE IS NOT GUARANTEED.

By Order,

ERNEST R. COOPER, Secretary.

Company's Office,
1 Market Place, Southwold.
14th April, 1904.

THE SOUTHWOLD PRESS, PRINTERS, 6-8 CHURCH STREET, SOUTHWOLD.

Although most of the papers relating to the River Blyth Ferry Company were destroyed, accounts are available from 1901 onwards and Bernard Segrave-Daly has looked into them. He noted that Edward Octavius Denny, a military friend of Ernest Adnams in a division of the Norfolk Volunteers of the Royal Artillery was the auditor, and he has picked out the following information.

By 1901 the company had accumulated some £356 in undistributed profits. Its assets were:

Dock and Wharf	£307
Pontoon and Boat	77
Engine	38
Investments	200
Cash reserves	234
Total assets 1901	£856

The ferry, bound for Southwold

In 1901 the rent on the land on the Walberswick side was £16 increasing to £36 the next year and it increased every few years to £88 in 1920 and £199 in 1929. It was paid annually to Mr Rix of Beccles who was the agent for the Blois Estate. Wages went up more slowly, starting at £84 in 1901 and increasing to £104 in 1915. They were over £200 by 1920.

The 20% dividend was maintained for fifteen years as expenditure remained static but income continued to grow, but this was thanks to a government subsidy. In 1916 it no longer covered costs and a loss was made for the first time, causing the investors and directors to take a cut. The dividends went down to 10% and the directors, who had been taking £25 for themselves in fees, reduced it to £20. Worse was to come as the local fishing industry declined, causing much of the associated workforce to go elsewhere, and dreadful storms affected the operation of the ferry itself. No fees or dividends were paid over the next four years.

And of course, in the meantime Britain had found itself in the midst of war.

Chapter four

Ferrymen Cross: father and son

Benjamin Cross, born in 1837 to James and Elizabeth, was a fisherman first and foremost, absent from the Blything census in 1861 when he was in Northumberland on board the Ellora, and he was away at sea again when the official recorder came round in 1881. His wife Rachel (nee Howard) would take care of the home and family in those times: they had nine children, although sadly their three eldest daughters died at a young age including two in the same year, 1874, suggesting that they may have succumbed to a contagious illness.

There were three more daughters and three sons including Weston Albert who was born in 1866 and would be destined for work on the ferry.

Perhaps it was partly due to the harshness of life on the open sea, combined with the hardships and tragedy going on back home in Walberswick that made Benjamin take up the offer of a job on the ferry. It seems that he started out by helping the ageing George Todd on the rowing boat, and some of the stories later attributed to Todd may actually have involved Cross, and vice versa. Benjamin was almost thirty years younger but he too sported a fine beard and he had many choice sayings of his own.

Todd had been laid off by the time the new chain ferry was brought in and Benjamin was the main operator, pulling the cord to make the whistle shriek in order to let everyone know that it was about to make its way across the river. As passenger numbers steadily increased, the shrieking whistle sounded time and time

Benjamin Cross with the old rowing ferry

Benjamin Cross

again throughout the day. He was kept busy and certainly he earned the two-guinea bonus that the directors of the River Blyth Ferry Company bestowed on him in the early years.

Ben Cross became a portly man with a knowing glint in his eye, and he developed a barrel-shaped midriff that gave away his liking for a pint and a yarn. In the first few years of the new century, the decaying Southwold Harbour had become a focus for attention once more as the burgeoning herring fishing industry saw many of the Scottish drifters sent down from the packed port of Lowestoft to its near neighbour. Southwold, unable to cope, had to be rescued by new owners and investors.

Now there were gutting stations, pickling plots and market offices, a processing house known locally as The Kipperdrome, not to mention a large number of foreign-sounding women: the Scottish herring girls who followed the fleet. From photos taken at the time, it seems they made good use of the ferry, and no doubt a few of them had a smile and a wink for the bemused ferryman.

Scottish fisher folk on board the ferry around 1907–12

Benjamin now was looking towards retirement and his son Weston, known as Wessy would be his natural successor. Wessy had also been a fisherman on boats such as The Amigo, The Ester and Pride of the Cliff until around 1887. He was a skilled boatbuilder, renowned for his carbol and clinker built boats and the famous yacht designers DeQuincy and DeCorsy worked with him, sending Atlantic racing boats for him to service, often before they set off for Cowes. He cut back on this work when he became ferryman proper.

Wessy Cross would soon be honoured to operate the ferry for a very special passenger in 1906: the Princess of Wales came to the area on 30th October and in the following photograph he is seen trying to hold open the gate for the Princess's car to disembark, while saluting and perhaps also holding on to his hat in what appears to be a stiff breeze, judging by the flags. No red carpet for Her Royal Highness on this occasion – the water is lapping over the pontoon ramp as the motor car rolls off.

Everything changed with the advent of war and once again the North Sea did not seem like enough distance between Suffolk and her European enemies. Southwold was in the direct path of German Zeppelins headed for London and it was at severe risk of landing parties and invasion. The tourists fled, although Belgian refugees came in their place, and ferryman Cross may have been scratching his head as he tried to make sense of the incomers' language. Army units came and went too, some bringing cycles, some with horses, and some brought a brass band.

The town was attacked, first from the air and then by bombardment from a submarine – many shells fell on the marshes and some must have been too close for comfort to all those people living and working in the area. The ferry remained busy and in 1918, even before the war had ended, visitors started returning.

As if being full-time ferryman wasn't enough, Wessy was becoming something of an all-round entrepreneur, hiring out sailing boats and rowing boats to the public so that they could 'mess about' by themselves on the river. One can only assume the tides were much kinder in those days.

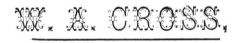

W. A. CROSS,

FERRYMAN.

WALBERSWICK.

SAILING & ROWING BOATS FOR HIRE.

REASONABLE CHARGES.

Weston Cross's business card

A woman boards with a pram, early 1900s

Weston may have swapped a harsh life on the open sea for a seemingly quieter one down on the River Blyth, but it was by no means an easy option to take. At that time the service would often start at 4am so that local tradesmen could bring their deliveries across. Newsons bakery was based in Southwold, opposite where the museum is now, and their deliveries would come over by pony and trap, whatever the weather.

Not only did the ferry start early, sometimes it would run very late in the evening to bring home the fishermen who had been working out of Lowestoft. Both Benjamin and Wessy had sympathy for these hard-working men and if they didn't take the chain ferry across they would make the trip by good old-fashioned rowing boat.

Wessy had married Susannah Rhoda Sagin, a Southwold girl, in 1891, and soon they started their own large family of five girls and three boys – the last two, James and Weston junior, were twins. However Susannah took an active part in helping her husband with the ferry, bringing lunches and beer down to the ferrymen every day that she could. She would clean the ferry in the evenings and as her boys grew older they too helped on the boats. Each boat that Weston made was named after one of his children, including those called Cathleen, Pips, Gladys, Ethel, Jimboy, Wessyboy and Sonnyboy.

Weston 'Wessy' Cross

Wessy on board the pontoon ferry

As his father Benjamin enjoyed a well-earned retirement, Weston started working with his cousin Bob Cross, who was the son of Benjamin's brother William. Soon the next generation were helping too, rowing the gentry on the river in good weather, and by the time Benjamin died in 1920, the ferry service was already in safe hands.

Crossing towards Southwold with a wagonette and foot passengers pre 1914

Lady Stradbroke takes a trip across the Blyth with ferryman Wessy, 1939

Chapter five

The River Blyth Ferry Company – the final years

In the early 1900s Ernest Adnams had to take a step back from his business dealings, since he had been diagnosed as having a brain tumour. In about 1909 he moved to a sanatorium in Surrey but he still liked to return to Southwold to keep an eye on the brewing firm – he was still collecting his director's fee and when he saw in the company records that it said he had been removed from office under the Lunacy Act, he furiously crossed it out.

However, his name disappeared from the records of the River Blyth Ferry Company and J J Mayhew, a Lacons Bank Agent, Southwold town Mayor and supporter of the Southwold Railway, became Chairman. In fact virtually all of the directors of the ferry company were Aldermen or Mayors of the Southwold Borough at some time, with a succession of local solicitors taking the role of Secretary, an exception being W G Bridal, former station master at Southwold.

By 1911 the honeymoon period between the local townsfolk and the ferry company was well and truly over – in that year the Government's Board of Trade Harbour Department received strong complaints about the inefficiency of the service. One of the problems was weather, another was the tides, but it was the good old silt that was causing particular trouble, and as it built up yet again, the ferry would become prone to grounding, its engine struggling to haul it through the treacherous river bed.

Trade should have been increasing, helped by the new railway extension down to Southwold Harbour and Blackshore

Quay. Unfortunately, this opened in 1914 just as the local fishing industry was on the brink of collapse and Britain was heading for war. But the ferry managed to keep going, and make a profit until its first loss in 1916 as mentioned previously.

Tradesmen still used the service regularly and the picture below shows a trade ticket that could be renewed annually at a cost of £1, allowing an errand boy to cross on foot. However, it does state that the service is not guaranteed.

REGULATIONS.

1. The Company reserve to themselves the right by their Servants or Agents to refuse to carry any traffic which in their opinion would involve extra risk by reason of its being of a dangerous or exceptional character or otherwise.

2. The Landing Stage is the property of the Company and may not be used for other boats except by permission.

3. The Company will not be responsible for injury to persons, animals or things while using the Pontoon and this is a condition of the issue of this ticket.

4. The hours of traffic are as follows :—

	Sundays.	Week-days.
July, Aug. and Sept.	8 a.m. 9 p.m.	7 a.m. 9 p.m.
Remainder of year	8 a.m. 8 p.m.	7 a.m. 8 p.m.

The Pontoon service is not guaranteed.

NOT TRANSFERABLE.

RIVER BLYTH FERRY COMPANY,
LIMITED.

TRADE TICKET
FOR

Errand Boy on foot.

N.B.—This Ticket must be produced on demand.

All year round the pontoon was taking a battering, and amounts of around £25 a year appear in the accounts for repairs. However in 1901 the figure was more than £87 for repairs to the pontoon and engine, in 1904 there were also repairs to the rowing boat, and a new driving chain was needed. The following year an additional cost of £14 was shown for overhauling the pontoon, dredging and painting, and more dredging at £85 took place during the next year, as well as the construction of a concrete wall.

The struggles continued: more overhauling, and more new chain, although the Ferry Company did make 8/6d out of selling the old chain and some spare wood. Modifications were needed from time to time to improve the approach and slipways, and in 1911 the pontoon was fitted with a new prow and gates at a cost of £27. In the balance sheet under the heading 'assets,' the pontoon and boat are valued at just under £9.

The ferry was making a loss by the end of the First World War, even though the government grant had gone up to £220 by 1918, while income from tolls had declined to £150. It is most likely that the military men who were stationed in the area made free use of the service but didn't pay any fares – this certainly happened in the second war.

When the tourists returned in 1919 the income from fares went up dramatically to over £568 but still the balance sheet shows a deficit, with costly repairs and general costs escalating. The directors agreed to spend out on a new boiler in 1925, it cost the hefty sum of £60 but in presenting the following years accounts, new chairman John Joseph Mayhew said it had justified itself in that the bill for coal had gone down considerably as a result.

He added, 'Considerable difficulty has been experienced in keeping the engine going at times, but through prompt assistance when required, and care in driving, the year has passed without any serious damage to the takings. Repairs etc, it will be noticed, are down nearly £130.'

Ending on a note of gloom, he warned, 'The time for a new

engine and probably a new pontoon is near, and enquiries as to the former are on foot.'

Mayhew had commented that during the whole of the summer there had been industrial unrest which had made itself felt in every business throughout the Kingdom – there had of course been a General Strike in May that year, but we can assume the ferrymen didn't take part. Mayhew was pleased to say that money from tolls that year had been 'the second best in the history of the company.' But they still made a loss.

The accounts for 1927 are missing, but it is known that on 19th April a replacement pontoon was towed down from Lowestoft port behind the tug boat 'Dispatch.' The old pontoon was taken away on the same tide to be broken up for scrap.

The gleaming new ferry, named The Blyth, was 62 feet long including ramps and 17 feet wide. It had been built by John Chambers and Son Ltd; the cost is not known, but is thought to have been around £1,000 judging by the value after depreciation recorded in 1928. The ramps were controlled by a winch driven from the main engine, which was a heavy duty, single cylinder marine slide valve engine, directly connected to the main Gypsy wheel drive and clutch operated. Steam would be provided from the 'donkey' boiler alongside.

The improved design was capable of carrying up to two tons of vehicles or other loads plus 20 passengers. It had distinctive stanchions and one of its passengers would later be amazed to discover that it had a 'twin' – he had boarded an identical ferry that was being run spasmodically across the Suez Canal – even carrying camels.

Back at home, Mayhew commented in his Chairman's report, that although takings had been maintained at a satisfactory level, 'There have been heavy items of expenditure incurred in connection with the service which have so depleted the profits as to render it inadvisable to declare a Dividend in excess of 10 per cent, less tax...'

New Southwold–Walberswick pontoon ferry The Blyth, late 1920s

It seems that the ferry company had realized a new source of income, albeit a relatively small one: they made £5 out of advertisements carried on the ferry.

Nearby, the Southwold Railway faced disaster as newly-instituted bus routes began to strip the quaint service of its income. With only one week's notice, the line closed in April 1929, causing shock and concern. Even so, in the early 1930s, the directors of the ferry company had no idea that their own service was entering its final years. They invested in a larger engine-house, and agreed to have welding carried out during a major overhaul of the equipment. Edgar Pipe took over as chairman after the death of J J Mayhew, and he was pleased to see that in spite of adverse weather conditions the income remained good. In 1931 the pontoon made 26,843 journeys, while in 1933 176,787 tickets were issued.

By 1937 the profit and loss account was back in the black, even though costs were still rising and income from tolls had gone down. The equipment was being maintained to a high standard and there was no reason to suspect that the chain ferry's days were now numbered.

The coming of the Second World War was a terrible blow for all concerned, but in Southwold and Walberswick, they too felt its effects at an early stage. In 1939 the Army arrived to put paid to any of Hitler's ideas about invading from the North Sea, and as part of their legitimate vandalism they blew up the disused railway bridge.

Meanwhile there were alterations being carried out in the harbour which resulted in worsening conditions further up the channel. Nature seemed to take delight in its modified access route, and wave action scoured the river banks right up to the slipway approach, eroding it so badly that a concrete wall had to be built on the Southwold side along the edge of the nearby dyke to avoid flooding. A few years later the County Surveyor reckoned that the general foreshore level had been lowered by an average of two feet. By then the access and slipway for the ferry was no more.

For a short time the chain ferry continued to operate and it remained popular, but its passengers weren't always well-behaved. One local lady recalled that soldiers who were stationed at Walberswick used to go across to Southwold on a Saturday night and get drunk, so that very often knives would be drawn. Not only that, they weren't paying for the trip.

In August 1940, with little income and constant outgoings, the service was suspended. The following January, MP for Lowestoft South and chairman of Adnams and Company Ltd, Pierse Loftus made a complaint in parliament, asking the Secretary of State for War whether the War Office was prepared to pay for the heavy daily use of the ferry by its men from November 1939 to the point of closure, because, he said, all vehicular communication had now been interrupted, causing grave inconvenience and increased use of petrol owing to a nine mile journey that now had to be taken by road to get to the other side of the river. Loftus was naturally concerned for the ailing fortunes of the River Blyth Ferry Company, in which Adnams still held a 10% stake, but also he was standing up for the local communities.

In reply, Captain Margesson stated that it was a question of Crown exemption, but on this occasion the War Office was prepared to pay half. The ferry never resumed, and the army dismantled the chains and anchorages and moored the pontoon in the middle of the river. With the fierce tides and changing riverbank, the ferry, dragging at her moorings, drifted and settled in the mud.

Now the communities were finally cut off from each other. As former secretary Leonard Septimus Harrisson later said in Janet Becker's book *The Story of Southwold*, 'The Company suffered abuse and derision in its time, but its loss has been, and still is, severely felt by residents and visitors to both Southwold and Walberswick.'

In fact a service of sorts would quickly be up and running again with the ferrymen taking to the rowing boat once more. Sadly, there was no helping the company, although the directors seemed to be holding out for a possible resurrection of the pontoon once the war ended. The final blow came in 1942 when the then landowner Sir Ralph Blois refused to renew the licence. The company had no choice but to go into liquidation.

In February it was wound up and later the pontoon would be salvaged for scrap, but the company still managed to pay £17. 10s for each of the £10 shares outstanding, which wasn't a great deal of profit for the 57 years worth of investment that some such as Adnams had made in the River Blyth Ferry Company.

Chapter six

Old Bob Cross – teller of stories

Ferryman Robert (Bob) Cross was a Walberswick man through and through. He was born in the village in 1873 to William Cross and Ann (nee Cullingford); he had nine siblings. For a time he was educated at the little local school by Mrs Starling who for 3d per week would teach the local children their 'Three Rs.' Leaving there at eleven he became a marshman, looking after a large herd of cattle on the old town marshes. His job included counting the 200 cows at 7o'clock in the morning then checking them again at 6pm to ensure none had strayed towards Dunwich.

He met his wife-to-be Hannah in Walberswick while she was in service for a family from London who came to the little Suffolk beauty spot on holiday each year. Hannah was from Hornchurch in Essex but she must have fallen for Bob's charms for she agreed to come and live in Walberswick as his wife. They married in her home town in 1907 and they had two children named Constance (Connie) and Cyril (Young Bob).

'Old' Bob Cross

After marrying, Bob was involved in building their family home which was given the rather grand name Ocean View. In fact it stands on the Green in front of The Bell Inn, although it is possible to see the North Sea from the tiny bedroom window upstairs. The terraced cottage is still occupied by Bob and Hannah's granddaughter, Hazel Church.

Being raised so close to the river, it was inevitable that Bob would have a love of boats, so the job of fisherman lured him. He firstly fished out of Walberswick on the 'Prima Donna', owned by a local man named George English, then he went on to fish on the bigger boats out of Lowestoft which had crews of up to ten men. These boats would follow the mackerel shoals west down to Cornwall and it was there that in 1896 he was involved in the famous Newlyn Riots. It was because their fish had been caught on a Sunday, breaking an ancient local law, that Newlyn fishermen boarded the Lowestoft boats and emptied them of their catch. The fighting had to be broken up by troops as it was so violent.

Bob began his ferry career in 1903 when his uncle Benjamin Cross, then aged 65, retired. When he wasn't away fishing, Bob worked part time with his cousin Wessy Cross on the steam ferry, and he continued until it was laid up in 1940.

After the pontoon ferry ceased to operate, the important link between Walberswick and Southwold was broken. Bob kept the service going mainly for the use of the military but of course also for the villagers. Many of the troops were stationed in Walberswick and they were keen to cross over to Southwold in the evening as there was plenty more going on there for the young men, especially the cinema and the larger variety of hostelries. Some of the men were rowdy passengers to say the least, and most of the time the soldiers didn't pay.

When Sir Ralph Blois refused to let the ferry continue from his land, the River Blyth Ferry Company was forced to admit defeat and give up, but Bob had other ideas. He enlisted his brother Ernie to help him and together, using a fishing boat, they resurrected the old rowing boat service, except they moved it about 50 yards upstream and on to Parish land, where it operates today.

Opposite: Bob Cross

Bob Cross carrying the tools of his trade

Later a council official, from the County Surveyor's office no less, would come and take a look at what was going on, and make a full report. In it he said, 'Evidently, the present service was inaugurated by an unsignified arrangement between the local folk at Walberswick and the Ferryman. There appears to be no stated agreement to perform, nor any official or statutory supervision.'

This was surely outrageous in the eyes of the authorities. With an almost tangible shudder the inspecting engineer wrote, 'The service is operated on the basis of "when anyone wants to go over" and is normally run between 7am and 6pm, the Ferryman deciding what hours he will suspend the service whilst he takes his meals. Outside these usual hours he will operate by special request.' (As we will see later, this could simply be when someone shouted from the opposite bank.)

In an almost incredulous tone, the man adds, 'Sunday service is operated in fine weather and during such hours as may be expedient (or lucrative), but the Ferryman claims that he and his relief are entitled to some time off each week.'

Clearly the latest breed of ferryman had lost none of the early skill of Todd in delivering some fine retorts.

Business must have been doing well, in spite of the ad hoc nature of running it. A new corrugated iron ferry shed with a tortoise stove to keep the ferrymen warm was built on the Walberswick side, and some rough jetties were constructed on either side of the river bank. In fact, the ferry was open all year round at this time and on cold days Bob and /or Ernie would sit in the shed in front of the stove with just a small window they opened and closed to check if any passengers were waiting.

The ferry shed was something of an Aladdin's cave. Passers- by would love to just peek inside. A display board informed all comers that the cost of the passage was now 'tuppence per person, all at their own risk'.

Local boat builder William (Weary) Page was instructed to build Bob his new ferry boat, which Bob named the Shirley R

Cross, after his first granddaughter. Naming your boat after a member of the family was something of a tradition. Bob was a committed family man and helped his daughter Connie raise her three children in his house as her husband died even before the birth of their last child, Hazel.

Bob was something of a gruff character, but he had his charms. Often he would borrow items from the users of neighbouring huts, and when some time later they realised they needed their very useful tool or piece of equipment, they knew where to look first – it might well be lurking in Bob's shed.

Bob loved to smoke a pipe and it was rumoured that he would even stuff shredded rope in it and smoke that when times were hard. His granddaughter Hazel remembers he would sit in the corner of the kitchen and puff away so much that the family couldn't see to the other side of the room. Not a man of fine manners, he was also known to drink tea straight out of the spout of the teapot

When Bobs' daughter first acquired a television he refused to watch it and would never go into the sitting room when it was on. He preferred to sit alone in the kitchen, puffing on his pipe, whilst listening to the radio.

Bob's days out at sea had left him with two fingers missing. The accident had occurred when he was poisoned by a weaver fish whilst hauling in the nets at sea. His little finger and the one next to it eventually turned gangrenous, so just the stumps of the fingers were left on one of his hands. Customers were amazed that he could row so skilfully with so little to grip on the oars.

Opposite: Bob Cross with friend Charlie Gilbert

He was not much of a conversationalist but he did like to spin a good story, the most famous one of all was about the travelling circus which came to Walberswick Now, there are so many variations on this theme that it will feature at length in a later chapter, but in Bob Cross's version, he swore that the circus had one day arrived by mistake at Walberswick instead of Southwold. Bob and Wessy were persuaded to take the two elephants together across on the chain ferry as they would not be parted.

Sitting outside his ferry hut with a pipe in one hand, Bob would insist, 'That nearly sank the ferry, level with the water she was.' The amazed audience might just catch the twinkle in his eyes as he recounted this story, among others, time and time again.

The following story may well have been told by Bob, but here it comes from a letter printed in the East Anglian Daily Times in August 1988 when C W S Hurr, a former secretary to the River

Old Bob (left) and a friend enjoy a yarn

Blyth Ferry Company reminisced about how he used to have to cycle to the ferry every Saturday morning to collect the week's takings, which usually comprised a small sack of copper pennies and half-pennies. He then had to balance it on his cross bar and walk back to the office to count it. He revealed, 'I also well remember that dear old blind organ grinder and poet, W S Montgomery from Westleton, with his donkey-drawn barrel organ. This intelligent animal would start from home, arrive at the ferry and stop. Mr Cross would see him safely over, and it would then proceed to Southwold market place and stop, all entirely unaided by its blind master.' (The writer doesn't say, but presumably it was the master who paid the fare!)

Bob no doubt enjoyed this little ritual, for he certainly had a way with animals. He was one of the many ferrymen who have had dogs for companions on the boat, and he also used to keep and breed geese down at the ferry so that the family could have their eggs. When the goslings were small, Bob used to bring them home in case the coypus or foxes might take them, and the tiny, awkward, fluffy creatures would sit in the kitchen whilst the family ate their meals. Nobody minded.

The ferry geese were something of an institution and a postcard was even published with them on. Customers were not always keen on the geese though, as they frequently had to dodge the fearsome, flapping birds, and some would be chased clean away.

Bob was also very fond of a seal that used to sleep on the deck of the chain ferry at night. The seal would fish and dive about in the river and sea during the daytime but as soon as the signal was sounded for the last ferry, the seal would unfailingly appear to take up its bedtime position on deck. People would come to Walberswick just to see the seal, it was quite a spectacle.

In 1956 at the age of 83, Bob found that the tides and rowing had become too much for him and he took a step back from the ferry letting his son, 'young Bob' and grandson David take over the service.

He still acted as Fen Reeve for the Walberswick Common Lands Charity, so he would carry on walking along the dyke wall daily to count the cattle, but the rest of the time he would sit among the boats or in his hut down at the ferry, just watching or spinning a yarn with friends.

Bob Cross was able to enjoy being among those he loved, as well as his beloved boats, right up until his death in 1968 at the age of 88.

Chapter seven

Ernie Cross 'Quiet but so charming'

Ernie Cross worked on the chain ferry for a short time just before it was laid up, then helped his brother Old Bob Cross a few years later on the rowing boat service. Ernie was Bob's younger brother, he was born in 1884. Ernie is described as having a very different personality to his brother Bob. To look at he was taller and thinner than Bob, but he still sported the very significant 'Cross' moustache.'

People say he was a quiet man who rarely said much but when he did he had quite a charming character.

He married local girl Elizabeth 'Bessie' Moore in 1911 and she was quite the opposite to himself. She was a shortish, stout lady who had plenty to say. As people commented, 'What little Ernie said, Bessie certainly made up for it.' Others called her 'a real spitfire.'

Right: Ernie Cross

The couple lived on the Green and had two children, Winifred (Winny) and William (Billy or Tiddler). Neither of their children went on to have offspring themselves, but Tiddler, so nicknamed because he was short and stocky like his mother, did later marry a woman who already had a child.

Ernie loved to keep geese down at the ferry and when people complained about their behaviour he simply said that they were there as 'visitor management.'

Ernie had quite a volatile personality and he was easily wound up. 'He would chase you up the road if he was cheated out of tuppence on the ferry' one former customer recalled.

Ferryman Ernie Cross, c.1950

Another anecdote comes from Vida Connick, who recalls an event which happened during the war, when the old pontoon ferry lay derelict in the mud, and the rowing boat service had finished for the day. A would-be customer had been drinking, and wanted to cross the river. Vida says, 'One summer evening, my husband Richard and I walked down to the river, and when we got there, we saw a man on the other side who had come from Southwold. He walked along the landing stage and he kept looking across, he said a few swear words, and said "There's nobody to bring me across the river, so I'll swim." He pulled his trilby hat on tight, took off his shoes and tied the laces round his neck and started to swim.'

The man soon got into difficulty. Vida says, 'As he got nearer to the old ferry, the current was so strong that he couldn't make it. He started saying "Help!" so Richard went in and helped him out. He got up to the road as Ernie Cross came round the corner. This drunken man swore at him and said "You didn't bring me across so I'm not paying you." He got a handful of coins out of his pocket and threw them in Ernie's face.'

'Ernie only got a little cut but he was angry then – he was only a little man and this was a big man, but Ernie clenched his fists and rushed up and gave him a big thump on the back.' They all went their separate ways, although Vida adds with amusement that one of the residents quickly came out to look for the pennies that had rattled on to the road.

Ernie worked on the ferry until the early 1950s. The rest of the time he worked as a general labourer in and around the village. When he died in 1954 his wife Bessie told everyone later that she knew something bad was going to happen as there were lots of robins in the garden just before it happened. How strange.

Chapter eight

Ruby Canham: 'A bit of seawater will never hurt you'

Ruby Canham, nee Cooper, was Southwold's first known ferry lady. She was born in Reydon in 1910 to fisherman Charles Cooper and his wife Florence, nee May, and the family moved to Walberswick when she was three. Charles had started as a cook on the trawler 'Faith' but later went on to become a skipper. During the First World War he was away at sea on minesweepers, then when he came home in 1918 he bought his own long-shore fishing boat and worked out of Southwold Harbour.

Ruby, in an unpublished memoir, said, 'He was also a crew member of the Southwold lifeboat, which at that time used sail and oars, they had no engine until years later when a gentleman donated a motor lifeboat in memory of his wife, which was called Mary Scott. We used to get up in the night when the gun went off. I have seen them go out in terrible weather.'

Ruby grew up around boats, often going out to sea with her dad and learning about the different methods for catching lobsters and crabs or herring and sprats. Naturally the family ate a good deal of fish, although Ruby remembered the whelks being tough and 'not very good for the digestion.' As an adult she liked to cook fish until the skin burnt, and her own son still remembers the evocative smell today.

As a young girl Ruby's love of the sea was shared by her friends at school and they would sneak off to go paddling in summer time, for which they were caned on the hand. Adults were all too aware that living near the river, sea and marshes had its dangers, and although Ruby never spoke of it, her family believe that she knew of children who had drowned in the area. Ruby herself had fallen off a plank and into the marsh when only about seven and she was lucky that there had been soldiers around to haul her out.

Ruby's mother gave her a hiding after that incident, for coming home covered in mud and weed. Florence Cooper had enough to do: she was cleaning and doing laundry for people in Walberswick and also taking in washing for the soldiers. In return the men gave her tins of corned beef and jam and rabbits, which must have made a welcome change. The family never went hungry.

The Coopers had two homes: in winter they lived in Tows Cabin near to the Bell Inn, then in summer they moved to a large black fishing hut down by the river, probably so they could rent their house out to visiting artists. Both properties still stand and the hut, called The Savoy, is worth a great deal more now than it was then. In Ruby's youth it was built on stilts and the family would have a rowing boat tied up outside so that if the tide came up especially high they could step straight out of their door and into the boat.

The Savoy at Walberswick

Ruby's son Dick Canham remembers her talking about those days in the old shack. He says, 'They didn't have much furniture downstairs, only a table and chairs. When the water rose, it came right up through the floorboards – they used to take up the carpets and move upstairs until it went down again.'

The Savoy is right next to the ferry and Ruby seemed destined to help out on it. Her dad bought a boat for her and her brother to share but her brother showed no interest in it and mostly Ruby had it all to herself. Her father used it to row out to his fishing boat called the Six Sisters, to check on sea conditions before putting out.

In winter Ruby helped her father to haul the fishing boats on to shore and to mend the nets. Being a practical girl she could make a sail out of scraps she found in his shed, and she could sail her little boat up the river. Her real love however was rowing.

Ruby left school at 14 and started work, helping her mother with cleaning studios and holiday homes, scrubbing floors for little money, but in 1926 she took over the evening ferry service when Cyril 'Bob' Cross went off to work as a builder in Essex.

For ten years she operated the service which ran from spring until September. She recalled, 'I loved to be on the river and I taught lots of visitors to row. Then in the evenings when the ferry closed I fetched people across the river. I was quite busy as there was quite a lot on in the summer.'

'Some went to Southwold for the evening and others came to Walberswick and at Trinity Fair time it was quite a big thing...they came from all the villages on their bicycles.'

I used to row them across and bring them back quite late sometimes, it was quite a big thing in those days as no-one had television or wireless; we made our own fun but it was lovely.'

Ruby wasn't a hard-hearted business woman by any means: she let people pay her whatever they could afford.

The image is idyllic but Ruby's son Dick tells of an occasion when Ruby slipped in the boat and fell, knocking her mouth hard on the side of the boat. He says, 'The doctor made her sit on the kitchen table while he pulled out the broken bits – no anaesthetic – but then they'd been army doctors, they'd been through the war and seen far worse things.'

Ruby's most oft-repeated story is rather more amusing. Dick says, 'When Ruby was living in the old shack by the river, the local vicar used to go drinking over at Southwold – I suppose he had it tough, everyone on at him and he liked a drink. He'd get drunk and stand at the river bank hollering late at night "Ruby, will you come and get me?" Her dad used to say, "Leave him, you don't want to go over there, he's drunk, you don't know what he might try." But she said, "If he tries anything I'll hit him with my oar!"'

That story has become a minor legend, and in one version the vicar did indeed proposition Ruby. But soon Ruby had a real love interest: a friend set her up to meet a young man named Frank Canham, and after that he would come courting, riding his motorbike, until five years later they married and moved to a smallholding in Holton.

Ruby had to give up the ferry but she remained busy, raising three children named Hazel, David and Richard (Dick), and helping her husband with his livestock, sometimes raising piglets in a box in the kitchen. The old Southwold Railway line ran through their garden, but it was silent now. The family had to drive back to Walberswick, which Ruby loved to do, taking her children to the seaside where she would often say, 'A little bit of seawater will never hurt you.'

Ruby and Frank, c.1935

     The Canhams would also go to Fritton Lake where Ruby could hire a boat and teach her children how to row. Even when she had joined an over 60s club she went on an outing with them to Fritton and rowed her friends all around the lake.

     Ruby's storytelling was only outshone by that of her brother Robert, nicknamed 'Dinks' Cooper. Dick says that Dinks never had to buy his own drink in a bar, he simply sat and regaled the visitors with his tall tales and they would be only too pleased to get the next round. One of his favourite stories, which even made it into the papers, was of how he had once fished up a lantern from old Dunwich, and the wick was still burning inside.

Ruby Canham worked hard all her life but did manage to slow down just a little in retirement, and looking back she had wonderful memories of her work and family. Her upbringing by the river, and a diet of fresh fish, must have stood her in good stead because she lived to the marvellous age of 93. She was right: a little bit of seawater had never done her any harm.

Ruby and Frank Canham

Chapter nine

Frank Palmer: 'You'll have to pay'

Born on St Valentine's Day 1884, Frank Palmer was something of a local celebrity before he became a ferryman.

In his youth he found that he had a talent for boxing, and he took part in light weight contests all over England. Sadly his parents strongly disapproved and so he wasn't allowed to take up an offer to train with a top coach, but he carried on with his sport regardless and fought against famous boxers of the time such as Sam Minto.

Frank Palmer (left) with sparring partner

He managed to go ten rounds with the black American champion fighter.

In those days the Assembly Rooms in Southwold were a popular boxing venue and Frank not only fought there but also helped to run the place. The worst blow he took was when, in his early twenties, his doctor told him that he had a weak heart and must hang up his gloves for good. Reluctantly he did so, at least for the time being, but such was his disappointment and shock that he ran away to sea.

Frank with young cousin Ernie Hurr 1911

Frank was the only son of Frank and Ann Palmer, he had four sisters, and his mother idolised him.

He grew up in Lorne Road, Southwold, which, says his daughter Mollie Robinson, was the 'upper class end' of town. His father had several boats but at first young Frank was apprenticed to a Mr Francis of Diss who was a cycle manufacturer. Mollie says of her father, 'He was the first in Southwold to have a wooden-wheeled cycle.'

But Frank, stunned by the pronouncement that he had to give up boxing, had become friendly with the Rogers family of Dunwich, and one of the sons, Sid, persuaded him to go and work on drifters, which he did as a mechanical engineer, no doubt to his mother's horror.

Frank worked on a number of boats, also taking cargo around England, Scotland and France. On one occasion he was arrested in Nantes, having gone ashore with a colleague who accidentally fell through a plate glass window, bringing the law down on them. They managed to bargain their way out of the cells.

Frank excelled at his work and at one time was put in charge of a dozen trawlers working out of Lowestoft. He married in 1914 and started his own family, setting up home at 7 Wymering Road, Southwold. Mollie says that her grandmother did not approve of his choice of a wife; Gladys Rogers was ten years younger than Frank and his parents did not think she was good enough for him. For one thing, her mother Isabel was a widow with 12 children – Gladys's father Edward had been a fisherman and in 1901 he had gone to sea in his boat named Clara, with his twelve year old son Esau to help him. In a stormy sea the boat had been overturned by a wave and Edward had struck out for shore, swimming with Esau clinging to his back. Father and son had tragically drowned.

Frank ignored all protests and married Gladys on 1st January; Mollie says the family always celebrated New Year more than they did Christmas. Also ignoring medical advice he would later take up boxing again, teaching his sons Frank and Patrick to box, and also Mollie herself. She recalls, 'He trained me in a shed, and he said "Now if ever a bloke accosts you, you can defend yourself."'

Frank and Gladys

In 1926 Frank came home from sea and began working on the steam ferry at Southwold, taking over from 'Old' Bob and Wessy Cross, and sharing duties with Arthur Brown. Their employer was The River Blyth Ferry Company, and when war broke out they were kept extremely busy carrying military men and equipment back and forth across the river, but without taking any tolls.

Cycling to work down Ferry Path

Eventually this would cause the whole operation to cease and director Pierse Loftus would raise the matter in Parliament, but for the time being the ferrymen were told they mustn't allow anyone else to cross without paying. Dutifully, Frank challenged the next fare-dodger, who on this occasion happened to be Anthony Eden, then Foreign Secretary but later Prime Minister. As Frank later told a reporter for the *Lowestoft Journal*, he declared, 'I'm not allowed to take people over without paying,' to which Mr Eden apparently replied, 'You're doing your duty. If everyone was as good as you we should be all right. Certainly we'll pay.'

Given Frank's prowess in the boxing ring, it seems unlikely that many people would have got the better of him, but of course women may have other means at their disposal. Frank would ruefully tell the story of how a young lady approached him one evening just as he was going off duty, and asked him if he would row her up the river on such a beautiful evening. Thinking he might earn a good bonus, Frank took her for a long guided tour.

He said, 'I pointed out all the places of interest and we stopped at an inn for a drink.' But Frank found that it was he who footed the bill (and she had a double white port), so then he rowed her back to Southwold, whereupon she hopped out of the boat without paying but, thanking him, said that she would like to do the same again.

The next evening the young woman did indeed appear, but Frank was wise to her scheme and he introduced her to a young man who was longing to meet her. Frank went home for his tea.

Being quick-witted, Frank took part in the rescue of a number of people and animals, and one event led to him having his portrait painted by well-known local artist R.A. Davison.

A young boy of about 12 years old was helping him on the ferry one evening when he walked off the end of the boat, carrying a bucket. It was dark and the first thing Frank knew about it was when he saw a hand sticking out of the river. Frank went after him and hauled him out, and, he said, 'He was still holding the bucket.' Frank didn't resort to the kiss-of-life to revive the boy: he said, 'I kicked him on the backside and he was soon all right.'

Once again Frank Palmer was the talk of the town, and in fact his own father had once rescued a woman from the sea and been awarded a medal for it. But Frank insisted, 'I didn't want all the bother of a medal or a certificate, so I had my picture painted instead.' That portrait, showing Frank in a noble pose, was not the only ongoing reminder he had of his heroic rescue; as the boy grew to manhood he would send Frank a 'little drop of something' each Christmas.

Frank continued as ferryman and Mollie says she used to cycle down to the ferry with her Dada's tea at four o'clock on a Sunday. At other times Ruby Cooper's mother Florence used to supply hot drinks to the ferrymen.

Mollie adds, 'He used to take me to meet a lot of famous people of the time: Peter Upcher the film star, Sir Robert Mostyn, and the Honourable Albert Holland were some.'

Frank Palmer with the portrait of himself

The chain ferry service came to an end and Frank went to work at Holton Aerodrome. After the war he went back to working on trawlers. It could be a gruesome catch; he said, 'We used to trawl up more dead men than you would find in a graveyard.'

But Frank could tackle any job with optimism and a good spirit. Even when, at the age of 75, he was employed to supervise the caravans and campers at the Southwold holiday site, he raised a smile and said 'What they will find for me next I really don't know.'

Frank Palmer, who was known by all to be 'strong as an ox', nevertheless was always a slim and lightly built man. He defied the doctor who had diagnosed a weak heart, but sadly his devotion to his special customers at the caravan site caused him to go out in bad weather while suffering from a cold. It developed into pneumonia and Frank died at the age of 78 on the 10th April 1962.

Chapter ten

The River Blyth Ferry Company –
the aftermath

To the people of Southwold and Walberswick, the fate of the
pontoon ferry named The Blyth was all too apparent. In the mid
1940s it lay desolate and decaying, half submerged in the mud by the
bank of the river after which it had been named. Once the war had
ended, the authorities began to take a serious look at what might be
done to resolve the problem

In July 1946 a letter was sent from the Clerk of East Suffolk County Council to the Clerk of Southwold Town Council, informing them that a report was underway but would not be available for some considerable time. Meanwhile, they felt that a temporary road bridge was needed, possibly at the site of the old railway bridge, or possibly where the ferry had run, in which case it would fall to the Borough Council to pay for it. Needless to say, this was met with a certain degree of hostility.

In replying, the Town Clerk said the proposal had been given careful consideration, and while every sympathy was felt for the provision of facilities that would help communication between Southwold and Walberswick, the Town Council could not support a scheme for a new bridge at the ferry site. Not only would it obstruct navigation of the river, they said, but it would cause inconvenience to fishermen and would preclude anchorage for craft in general. It was even suggested that the whole idea might be illegal. A temporary bridge at the former railway line was considered possible.

Now a long-time grievance was aired in that the Clerk added, in a nutshell, that the problem had arisen due to 'ill-advised and ill constructed works at the Harbour mouth,' which had been nothing to do with the Town Council and hence they didn't see why they should pay for a solution. The County Council was urged, politely, to get on with sorting out the Harbour mouth.

In the middle of the two councils was a Miss Dorothy Crichton of Walberswick, who was actively worrying at the respective clerks in a bid to get things moving. Her aim was to see that Walberswick did not remain cut off from Southwold and its facilities for much longer. Her well-informed and strongly worded letters helped to galvanise the authorities.

In March 1947 an engineer from the County Surveyor's office made a lengthy report, although some of his findings were admittedly short on fact, for the records of the River Blyth Ferry Company were by now incomplete. In the historical preamble it was stated that the service had ceased in 1939 and had been discontinued as a military necessity. More correctly, it added that the army had dismantled the chains and anchorages and had beached the pontoon, but the craft had been dragged by the force of the tides to its present position.

The situation was made worse by the fact that wave action had demolished the north bank slipway and lowered the foreshore level by two feet, so that any plan to restore the service would mean extensive work. As for the chains and anchorages, the surveyor said, 'these are 5/8" short link chain (probably calibrated) but I am of opinion they are no longer serviceable. The links are badly chafed and corroded in the "matings" and I suspect that after long immersion and strain the metal is tired.'

He added, 'The chain anchorages are completely demolished. This was done partly by the Military Authorities and has been completed by wave action and erosion.'

The bleak report continued with an assessment of the engine, boiler and working gear, which it said appeared to be, 'long past any economic repair.' Most of the time it had been under water for the past six years, it added, and moreover, 'The hull is flooded… the visible plating is in a very bad state and the frames and braces appear badly corroded.'

The 'Blyth' lying derelict at Walberswick

The report says that an unnamed local man who had at times worked on the ferry had told the engineer that for some years before 1939 the hull had been regarded as unsound and that the Board of Trade Inspector had demanded repairs and renewals to maintain the seaworthy condition of the craft.

After commenting about the ad-hoc ferry service that was currently being run, the engineer dolefully stated that any plans to revive the mechanized operation would require much more detailed inspections and calculations, but in any case the tides could swell so greatly now it could be positively dangerous. He said, 'Loading and discharging vehicles from the ramps at these times would be particularly hazardous, as the buoyancy lift of the ramps would be so excessive that a vehicle, half on the vessel and half on the slipway, if caught on the swell rise, would be in some danger.' He suggested that if the requirement to transport vehicles could be abandoned, a small and manoeuvrable boat could be used for foot passengers.

Miss Crichton had already said in a letter to the Town Clerk that the residents of Walberswick did not particularly want a vehicular service. They just wanted to be able to get across the river and enjoy the amusements and entertainments at Southwold, and catch a ferry back again. Even in the days of the pontoon ferry, this had ended at 8pm in winter and 9pm in summer, leaving them stranded unless someone would row them across.

An even more wide-ranging report was being compiled by a committee appointed by the Minister of Transport, which was looking at all the ferries in Great Britain. It started by defining what a ferry actually was, and commented that such a service was more than just an alternative to a bridge or tunnel, where it connected classified roads it should in fact be treated as part of the highway itself. Furthermore, it recommended that ultimately all such ferries should be free to use.

Looking specifically at the Southwold-Walberswick Ferry, the Ministry of Transport report came up with the recommendation that a vehicular ferry service should be restored if the navigational difficulties could be overcome, and in the meantime a temporary bridge should be erected. This was not news to anyone, and in fact by the time that report was published in 1948, a bailey bridge for pedestrians and cyclists only had been put in place.

Sadly there was no hope for The Blyth, and the following year she was sold for scrap. John Robert James, working for haulage contractors Coopers of Sweffling, had the job of re-floating the pontoon and dismantling it, and his daughter kindly donated the following photographs to the Southwold Museum.

John Robert James arrives with a large buoy and cutting equipment

The final demise of The Blyth meant a sad end to the dreams of local entrepreneurs, and it was a permanent loss for the communities of Southwold and Walberswick. It would now be up to local men and women to take up the challenge and provide a ferry service across the river for decades to come.

The following photographs of the pontoon ferry run by the River Blyth Ferry Company were taken in happier times.

Chapter eleven

Cyril (Bob) Cross: 'They say I could row before I could walk'

If you ever crossed the River Blyth by ferry in the 1970s to early 1990s, Bob Cross would almost certainly have been your ferryman. It was at this time that visitors began to flock to Walberswick and Southwold from all over the country and sometimes further overseas as travelling became easier. The ferry's role changed from a necessity to a novelty, making Bob a local celebrity. He was interviewed countless times by journalists and even had his photo printed in the New York Times. In 1998 when nearly 90 years old, he was interviewed by Sue Taylor and he spoke of his love for his life and the ferry, telling her that 'they say I could row before I could walk' which was probably very close to the truth.

Cyril Robert Cross was born in Walberswick in 1909 to Robert and Hannah Cross. The name Cyril was instantly dropped and he quickly became known to everyone as Young Bob. He spent his childhood in his home village and upon leaving school at 14 spent a year hiring out rowing boats on the river.

He told Sue Taylor, 'I had four rowing boats at one time and I used to let them out so people could row themselves up the river. If they couldn't row I took them.'

He also operated a night time service for the ferry from 9pm to 11pm after the chain ferry had shut. During this time he became friendly with many families who holidayed in Walberswick and at the age of 15 one family in particular befriended him. They were from Chingford in Essex and Bob said, 'Being from the town, they went mad when they saw the water!'

He rowed the children along the river, sometimes as far as Blythburgh, and his kindness was repaid when the parents offered to take Bob to London on a holiday for two weeks to show him the big city. The short stay ended up with a job offer in the family's building firm. His father encouraged him to seize the opportunity, as job offers such as that were few and far between in those days, and he was keen for his son to leave the village for a while to experience life outside Walberswick.

Young Bob stayed in the building trade in London and when war broke out he tried to enlist in the Navy but was refused as he was in a reserved occupation. He stayed behind during the Blitz, shoring up bomb-damaged blocks of flats and building bomb shelters 12 hours a day, 7 days a week. He worked until he was finally released from his reserved occupation in 1943 and straight away he enlisted in the Navy, first joining the battleship HMS Anson. After a year serving in the Atlantic, where the Navy were acting as cover for the Russian convoys, he asked for a transfer and joined the destroyer HMS Undine. Although a great sailor, after all that time at sea he was always seasick for a week when he returned to the boat after shore leave.

He certainly got to see the world beyond Suffolk, travelling to the Ice Fringe, the Far East and Australia, bringing back exotic gifts to his family on return. He was demobbed on January 12th 1946, and returned to Walberswick, where he worked as a fisherman for a year before returning to the building trade, first working for Henry Block, then Harvey and Leach in Lowestoft. Builders were desperately needed at this time to sort out the bomb-damaged houses in the area.

The ferry began to become a part of his life now that he was based back in Walberswick, and he used to help his father and Ernie on the ferry at weekends. He experienced the terrible 1953 floods and helped a neighbour just down the hill from his house battle to hold the door back to try and stop the floods from invading. In his spare time he was a keen fisherman, especially during the herring and shrimping season. On one occasion they caught so many herring the boat nearly sank with the extra weight.

Photos of 'Young Bob' Cross

Bob and his nephew David were famous for their kippers and bloaters which they smoked in their smokehouse down by the river. Orders for the smoked fish were always flooding in from appreciative villagers, as they were truly delicious. Bob also had a love of cars and his family remember having to accompany him for Sunday drives in his smelly uncomfortable motors that he was so very fond of.

Bob never married and he lived with his father, his sister Connie Church, and her three children in the family home, called Ocean View. Bob retired from the Building trade at 65 but continued his work on the ferry accompanied by his nephew David, who helped in his school holidays and weekends. Bob by then had his trusty dog Bonnie, a golden labrador-cross retriever who became almost as famous as he did. Bonnie was the ship's mascot, welcoming all passengers on board with her friendly face and waggy tail. She was especially popular with the children.

The ferry at this time was only open Whitsun to September, at weekends, although running seven days a week through the school holidays. There was no call for the service out of season anymore. When asked if he'd had any serious incidents he could only remember one, when a six year old boy toppled into the water after accidentally sitting on one of the lifebelts; luckily he was quickly fished out by his parents, shocked, soaked but unharmed. Bob commented that he himself fell into the river 'umpteen times- and I couldn't even swim'. He always had to rescue himself on these occasions.

One of Bob's favourite moments on the ferry was when a Scottish gentleman dressed in a kilt asked if he would object to him playing his bagpipes on board. 'I said I didn't so he did' laughed Bob, as he retold the story to Sue Taylor.

Bob loved his time as a ferryman, especially meeting the families who would return year after year. Like some of his predecessors, his face was recognised far and wide; he would remember with embarrassment that on one occasion whilst holidaying with his niece in Devon, someone spotted him even there as 'Old Bob, the Ferryman from Walberswick', and yelled out his name from a car window.

In 1970 Bob decided that it was time to have a new boat built and he turned to traditional boat builder William 'Weary' Page who had constructed the present boat, the Shirley Cross, at his shed in Walberswick. Based on the design of a Suffolk Beach Punt, the new boat would be able to carry nine people safely, and he fixed a stout hemp rope around to act as a fender, protecting it from striking the jetties as it came in.

Bob named his new boat 'Oud Bob' in honour of his father.

Bob tries out his new boat while in the background
David Church continues rowing 'Shirley Cross'

Above: William 'Weary' Page at his boatyard
Below: Bob with, 'Dubber' English, Freddy Eade and Bonnie the dog

Above: chatting with the famous storyteller 'Dinks' Cooper
Below: smiling at the doorway of his hut

Bob with his nephew and successor, David Church

Bob continued in his role as full-time ferryman until 1991 when he was the fantastic age of 82. He could still row then, but was worried about his job due to health reasons.

In his interview with Sue Taylor he explained, 'When you get old a heart attack or anything like that can come on sudden and before anyone could get to me, the boat could have drifted out to sea, I don't worry about myself but if you're responsible for other people you've got to think of them'

When asked about the future of the ferry Bob said he was confident, adding, 'it may be the space age but some people will always prefer travelling in the quiet old-fashioned way.'

His nephew David Church took on the full-time ferryman position as Bob stepped down from his job, so he could enjoy his retirement. After the ferry, Bob's life was taken up with his animals: he had two beloved cats which he would take for walks on harnesses, his dog Cassie, and he loved riding around Walberswick in his niece Hazel's pony and trap.

Above: Riding out with Hazel in the pony and trap

In his final years, Bob was never happier than when just sitting down at the ferry watching the world go by, chatting to visitors or tinkering around in his shed. He lived with Hazel up until his death in 2001 aged 91. A week before he died, he said to Hazel 'If I die tomorrow I have had no regrets, I've had a wonderful life.' What a lucky man!

Chapter twelve

David Church: 'Sandals for Sale'

When customers arrived to take the ferry in more recent years they were often surprised when the ferryman greeted them with a well educated accent instead of the gruff Suffolk voice they may have expected. David Church was born under the table in the family home 'Ocean View' during an air raid in 1942. Sadly, his father died when he was only two years old so he was raised by his mother Connie and his grandfather, 'Old Bob' Cross.

David spent his young childhood in Walberswick. One of his greatest lifelong friends Dennis Long recalled many stories of the capers they used to get up to when they were younger. 'David was one of the first children in the village to own his own wind up 'Dansette' record player. We used to pitch a tent on the Green outside Ocean View and The Bell, sit in it and listen to the same records over and over again. David's favourite record was Rock Island Line sung by Lonnie Donegan and he was a big fan of Tony Bennett too.'

Their tent exploits ventured further than this. When they were about eight or nine years old they pitched their

Young David, already in his element

tent near the ferry shed behind the Harbour Wall. Dennis says, When we were finally settled in for the night we found the roof of the tent was teeming in earwigs. We didn't lose heart and moved the tent round to another pitch but this was near the bottom of a hill.'

Unfortunately thunder and torrential rain struck and they got flooded out, but they stuck it out until morning, feeding off field mushrooms on the marsh for their breakfast. Dennis adds, 'we had lots of laughs'.

David and Dennis used to help Old Charlie Fisher and Bobby with their shrimping. Their job was to fill the copper up with water from the creek, light a fire under it and have it boiling before the men returned from sea. David often used to be in charge of keeping the smokehouse going for his grandfather and uncle too. The two boys were given the job of selling the shrimps from the corner seat outside the Gannon Rooms (now the village hall). They had a half pint pot and a pint pot which they would fill with shrimps at a cost of sixpence per pint.

They were also meant to sell the herring by walking from one end of the village to the other, but got wise to this and would just hang around the Green area selling them there, as they couldn't be bothered to walk that far. Some of the villagers complained to Uncle Bobby and Boco English that they never got a sniff of the herring, and the lads would get in trouble. The herring sold for one penny and one halfpenny each.

Sometimes the lads would go shooting on nearby land where they shouldn't. (Some might call this poaching!) They would hide their shoot in the bushes then sneak back for the birds when it was dark.

At school Dennis remembers that they would get served disgusting fatty lamb neck they used to call 'Brontosauraus'. They used to secretly fill their hands up with the food as it was compulsory to eat every last mouthful, then distract the teacher whist taking delight in flinging it in the fire to get rid of it. When David and Dennis were older they still used to giggle over the mischief they used to get up to, often reminiscing over a bottle of port at Christmas time.

David took to the oars at a young age

Another of David's 'partners in crime' was Chris Coleman, whose family first came from London on holiday in 1953. Chris and David were introduced, being of a similar age, and they hit it off straight away. The following year, Chris cycled down to Walberswick from London on his own so that he could stay with David's family and go off on more exploits. He explains the appeal; 'Walberswick had everything: it had the marshes and the sea – we were never indoors. We camped sometimes and David and I spent one amazing summer just living on a boat moored in the middle of the river. One of us would cook eggs and bacon in the morning; it was fantastic.'

When asked about the poaching episodes, Chris agrees that he also took part, commenting, 'In those days everyone did it. Even David's Uncle Bob had a walking-stick gun, a poacher's gun. David and I had guns from when we were 13 or 14, we'd shoot duck and pheasants.'

As well as being very much a village boy, Chris describes David as being a very well educated, very courteous and erudite man, adding, 'He was passionate about fishing, passionate about the river and the sea. They were very much his life.'

Above: David rows the ferry with Chris sitting in the bow

David as passenger with Chris at the oars

David attended Walberswick School until his 11 plus exam when he was quickly selected to apply for a scholarship for Framlingham College as he was achieving so well. He attained the 'all fees paid' scholarship and was shipped off to boarding school. It was such an achievement for a local lad in those days, to be given the chance to get a really good education and have the opportunity to take part in a wide range of activities he wouldn't have had the chance to do at home. It was surely here that he acquired that soft 'well spoken' accent.

Sport was a big part of his school life and he especially had a passion for cricket. Later on in life when he was full time on the ferry and couldn't watch the cricket as he was working, one of his prized possessions was a cricket cap with a built in radio given to him by a customer so he wouldn't miss out on the game. David progressed well at Framlingham College; his reports said he excelled especially in Nature Studies, and certainly he was most at home in the outdoors, but he also enjoyed reading, languages and especially geography.

Unfortunately as one of his teachers accidentally ran over him in their car when he was messing about in the school grounds, he lost all his front teeth so had to wear a plate for the rest of his life and he spent six months of his school days in traction due to a broken leg. Being in traction was extremely boring but he spoke fondly of his hospital days and he became quite a hand at card games during this time. He always made light and the most of any situation.

The good thing about being at private school was the extended holidays he used to get and it was in these periods that he began to help his grandfather Old Bob on the ferry. Being a ferryman in his school holidays was a great way of meeting lots of people and there was always a throng of friends hanging around the ferry hut, some of whom would give David a hand on the oars. Chris Coleman would often help David out, and having a good looking pair of young men, often shirtless, on the ferry attracted a great deal of attention from the young ladies.

Above: David with Old Bob's dog Trixie

Tourist attraction?
David (above) and friend Chris
(right) would often row without
shirts on hot sunny days

The ferry was fairly quiet during this time and there would always be time to swim and chat between customers. Chris recalls that although David had lost his father at an early age, he had plenty of male company and role models in his life, not least his grandfather, Old Bob. The ferry was like a magnet: men were always stopping by for a chat. In later years David would often go herring fishing early in the morning with his good friend Tiggy Knowland, whose wife Anne would cook them a big fried breakfast before David set off for a day's work on the ferry.

Still there was serious work to be done. After completing his A levels, the school encouraged David to continue on to university, but by this time he'd decided to follow his urge to travel and went off to Europe in a camper van with two friends.

On his return he moved back to 'Ocean View' and got a job in the accounts department at a coal merchants called Craskes in Lowestoft. Getting to work was always an adventure as he had no car, David and his sister Hazel often hitched together as she also worked in Lowestoft, but sometimes they were allowed to borrow the sooty sweeps van to drive home in. Eventually he bought his first car; having saved up fifty pounds he had a choice of buying a plot of land in Walberswick or a car – he chose the latter. Probably not the best decision financially, but definitely the most fun when you are a young man with a passion for cars except he wrote the car off on the sharp bends at Brampton Church almost immediately.

David met his love Julie English when he was 26 and they were married in 1972. Julie was also from Walberswick, she lived at 2 Albion Cottages next to the Anchor Inn. She was working as a secretary for Denny the Builders and through her employer the newlyweds were offered a house in Reydon. It meant migrating to the other side of the river but they did so and settled there happily, raising two daughters Daniella (Dani) and Polly. Polly is now a primary school teacher.

For the first time in years the ferryman didn't live in Walberswick.

Above: David with Julie
Below: with daughters Dani and Polly

David was offered a job with an agricultural installation firm, working on chicken farms. This meant travelling around the country a great deal and after a few years of doing this he set up on his own and started to employ many local people. As the business progressed the work took him world wide, working on farms in Martinique, Prague, Corsica and France.

David had a passion for travel, loving to meet and talk to new people whenever he could. He encouraged the family to travel and they went on many holidays. On a trip to Sweden he developed a love for skiing so many holidays were spent in the snow.

Above: the family in Guernsey
Right: a skiing holiday

Winter time was a good time for holidays as working on the ferry was always important during the summer months. Every weekend in the summer David would help his granddad Old Bob and later his Uncle, Young Bob work the ferry. In the period when Old Bob was getting too old to work and Young Bob was a builder he would run the ferry himself over the school holidays.

From the 1960s to the late 1980s David was famous locally for the leather sandals he used to hand craft. He would sell them from the ferry hut and each pair was made to measure.

To ensure your size was right he would draw around your foot onto a sheet of paper then transcribe it on to the leather sole. It was always the most wonderful sensation having him draw around your foot. The sandals eventually became too difficult to make due to the local leather merchants closing down and competition from abroad, but many people will tell you that no sandals will ever fit or feel like those ones did.

David's other interests included dabbling in a few car sales: he ran a car showroom in Southwold for a few years with a partner and then went on to run a car sales business.

As a keen wildfowler, he was a member of Walberswick Wildfowlers' Club and he attended regular meetings, enjoying the social side of it as much as the shooting.

He was a very practical man and he turned his hand to making a few gun cabinets among other metal work items. Most of all David loved sea fishing and as soon as the season and weather were right he would be out catching herring so that he could smoke them into his beloved bloaters and kippers.

He even adapted the fenders on the ferry stage so that he could leave his spinning rod in the water hoping to catch a sea bass whilst he rowed the ferry back and forth. He was very successful on a number of occasions; the family often had fish for tea. There was one time when, to the surprise of his passengers, he caught a cod with his bare hands mid stream whilst on the ferry.

David takes a break on the Walberswick side of the river

David became very involved with the local Reydon and Southwold Pantomime Group of which Julie was a member, and he helped by constructing and changing scenery. The cast always waited in anticipation of the fun pranks the scenery men would play during production. On one occasion in the last performance of Dick Whittington, when a storm was supposed to shipwreck the boat, bucketfuls of dried, smoked sprats rained down on the cast - thrown by David, Colin Upcraft and Michael Hackwell. They then fired water pistols, soaking one and all. David's voice could be heard coming from the wings, saying 'Sea's rough tonight' as the culprits roared with laughter. I often remember him having fits of giggles.

When his Uncle Bob decided to retire, David bravely took on the ferry business alone as no one else in the family was interested in the job. Whilst still running his agricultural firm, he worked on the ferry in the summer months then went back to the farms in the winter. Every ferry customer started to know him well as he was the only man taking the oars.

David had a genuine interest in all of his customers and he made many good and long lasting friendships from his time on the river. Television crews loved to come down and take footage of the ferry and David rowed a number of celebrities over the river while they were doing their various programmes: Maureen Lipman, Griff Rhys Jones and Jo Brand to name but a few. Some he liked better than others. He found loud, brash women a challenge, but being a well-mannered gentleman he had his own way of dealing with them, usually making some witty comment with a dead straight face, leaving them stepping off his adored ferry thinking about his words, then looking back to see the twinkle in his eyes and a wicked grin. Many of his quirky comments often referred to the air conditioning on the rowing boat, causing many an unwary passenger to think twice before realising he was joking with them.

Not being a big television fan, he often didn't recognise the many famous faces who crossed the river; no one was any different to him anyway, everyone was simply a friend or ferry customer to whom he would chat amicably. He was friendly with many of the fishermen, and one in particular said that after a bad morning or night at sea he was always cheered up by David's friendly greeting as they came back into harbour past the ferry.

Below: a long queue awaits – David treated all customers with equal courtesy

David had the ability to get along well with anyone whatever their origin or background. He had a good safety record on the ferry, the only fatality being a lady's pushbike which slid off the end of the jetty, full of shopping. It's not every day that grapefruits and packets of cornflakes are seen floating off up the river.

Above: David (centre) helping to mend fishing nets.

David always liked to create and try out new ideas. The first change he made to the ferry was installing new landing stages, changing from fixed stages to a floating pontoon system which moved up and down with the tide. The new idea worked well, as although very full of character and every artist's dream to paint, the old jetties were narrow and rickety and used to get very slippery due to the seawater washing over them. The new floating pontoons are wider and really stable, allowing passengers to pass each other, even with bikes and baby buggies; they are much safer.

The popularity of the ferry began to increase once more and so in 1996 David decided to have a bigger rowing boat built to replace the old ferryboat 'Oud Bob', which had been built by William 'Weary' Page of Walberswick in 1970.

The boat had given excellent service but it only took nine passengers and had a tendency to feel slightly unstable when 'larger' passengers were boarding. He instructed HMS boatyard at Southwold harbour to make him a boat of a similar design to the previous one, but which could take more passengers and would be more stable.

Gary Brown and his father Arthur Brown, experienced wooden boat builders, were drafted in to build the new ferry. Using Oud Bob as a template, they scaled up the measurements, made hardboard and plywood patterns and created the larger boat, much to David's satisfaction. Constructed of mahogany planking on oak frames, it had a thick hemp fender rope fitted all round to help protect against the constant knocks it receives as it comes alongside the jetties.

Once on a crossing, a customer had suggested to David that he could put an electric outboard on the back of the boat to help it along in strong tides. As the new boat was going to be heavier to row he decided to try out this idea and enlisted the help of a local electrician to set up a system so that the electric engine at the back of the boat could be operated by the rower at the front of the boat. They came up with the ingenious idea of a foot pedal so that the little engine could be switched on and off by the rower's foot whilst midstream if required. Having this little bit of help meant that the ferry could be kept open on the days when the wind and tide were usually unmanageable and the ferry would normally have to close.

The new ferry was named 'Halcyon Days' the first ferry not to be named after one of the family, but very apt nonetheless. It has proved to be a great success.

Facing page:
Arthur and Gary Brown
at work on the new boat

Right: Arthur prepares to
board the new boat

Below: the boat builders
take a ride:
(l to r) Roger Doy, Gary,
Phillip and Arthur Brown

Being a ferryman in the 1990s was not as straightforward as in previous years. Following the Marchioness disaster in London, new legislation came into force meaning that all persons carrying passengers needed to hold a Boatmasters Licence. This licence is issued by the Maritime and Coastguard Agency and involves an oral and practical examination, medical fitness certificate and regular attendance on a first aid course. Before this, anyone could take to the oars to help on the ferry, but now insurance won't cover you unless you are a certified Boatmaster 'Grade 3'.

David took the exam and agreed that it was time for me, his daughter Dani, to get involved as I had often expressed that wish. I took my licence in 1996. Although I only helped on occasions it was good back up for my dad on busy days and on Crabbing Sunday and Bank holidays we would sometimes work the two boats together, he always in Halcyon Days and me in Oud Bob, trying to keep the queues at bay.

During the late 1990s Walberswick and Southwold began to become extremely popular with day trippers and holiday makers alike and the ferry began to be busier than it had for a long time. Dad increased the opening hours on the ferry so it opened from Easter through until the end of October as demand increased. He was absolutely devoted to his role as ferryman, often working late to make sure everyone especially the elderly and families with young children always got back to the right side of the river before he closed up for the day.

In 1999 David finally purchased a Dell Quay Dory boat with outboard engines, something which he had always dreamed of having. He used the new boat primarily as a fishing boat, but also employed it as a very occasional ferryboat for when the weather was not suitable for rowing. The motor boat caused a bit of a stir within the ferry community as not since the Chain Ferry had a motor been used for the crossing. Passengers have however been very glad of this boat when the weather and tides have been appalling and the walk to the bridge would have been extremely uncomfortable. My dad loved his new boat.

Tragically Dad became ill in the year 2000 and was diagnosed with cancer which he quietly yet heroically fought until May 2001 when he died at the age of 59. His love for the ferry was so apparent when in the February half term before he died he even opened up the service using his motor boat so that he could see all his customers for one last time, none of whom knew he was ill as he hadn't told many people. He knew that the ferry would be carried on by me. He was a man truly dedicated to his family, friends and the ferry.

I am truly grateful to Simon Barnes for allowing me to quote the following extract from the obituary he wrote for *The Times*.

David Church
Cultured ferryman who turned a short river journey into a timeless experience

The Suffolk village of Walberswick and the town of Southwold are divided by the swift and quirky River Blyth. Since 1954 they have been united by David Church, who rowed the ferry between them from the age of 12. The road journey is a dozen or more miles, the walk via the bridge downstream takes 45 minutes. But for most of his life Church rowed people across in a couple of minutes with grace and aplomb and apparently effortless watermanship. ...It was once a reasonably leisurely task, but the huge increase in tourism has made the job of ferryman hugely taxing.

Ferry first-timers were often disconcerted by Church's educated, almost patrician, tones – not the salt-of-the-earth Suffolk voice they expected. He had won a scholarship to Framlingham College but left school to become an accountant with a firm of coal merchants. He gave that up and travelled around Europe in a Dormobile before coming back to Suffolk. He established a profitable business supplying chicken farmers, travelling widely in the ferry's off-season. But the ferry was the centre of his life.

There were three reasons why the ferry mattered. Church had a deep love of continuity and duty; a delight in conviviality and companionship; and an all-consuming love of the river, the sea, and the things that float on them.

He was the centre of the tourist industry in Southwold and Walberswick: the embodiment of calm travel and courteous manners. His genius was that he never got fed up with the tourists' endlessly repeated questions. Both the journey and the man added a dreamlike touch to every visit to this timeless place.

He was a devoted family man and leaves a widow, Julie and two grown-up children, Dani and Polly. The ferry re-opened after a celebration of his life had filled Walberswick churchyard with mourners who were unable to find a place in the overflowing church. The ferry will now be run by his daughter Dani.

Chapter thirteen

Today's Ferrymen

The team: (l to r) Butch, Luke, Nick, Crispin, Dani with son Charlie, and front: Digger and Nellie the dogs

Crispin Chalker - in his own words

'My first real memory of the ferry was simply passing the time of day, on occasion with David, as myself and a motley crew of canoeists passed the ferry stages, or boat, on our way out to sea. I have always loved open spaces, especially the sea and I think that played a role in myself and Dani getting to know each other, I find it quite amusing to think of the funny twists and turns in life, when one moment you are making a brief 'hello' to then being wrapped up in the internal workings of a rowing boat service, almost by accident.'

'I enjoy taking part in the rowing, on quiet days, but also muck in on busy days too. I didn't pay much attention at school, especially in maths lessons. I never did learn my times tables which is essential on busy days when a constant stream of bicycles, pushchairs, people of all shapes and sizes seem to come at you from every angle on the

stages! We had to replace the Southwold stage in 2007 and the Walberswick one in 2008. I really enjoyed building the pontoons in Wenhaston and then transporting them down to the ferry then putting them together and floating them up on the high tide. Our neighbour, a policeman, volunteered to give us a police escort with the first pontoons which made the whole exercise seem pretty grand!'

Above: Crispin and Butch rowing on the Thames in the Great River Race

Below: moving the new jetties

Adrian (Butch) Church

Butch grew up in Walberswick attending Walberswick primary school, then Sir John Leman High at Beccles. Leaving school in 1975 he went to train as a fabricator/welder at Richard Garrets Engineering firm (of steam engine fame) in Leiston for 5 years, At 21 finally he achieved his childhood dream of going to sea fishing for a living. He worked on boats 'Duchess' and 'Minerva' out of Southwold then 'Children's friend' which fished out of Lowestoft.

In 1983 he married Diane Muttitt also a Walberswick girl. Di is famous locally for her wonderful home cooking and baking. They have three sons, Tom, Bob and Sam. Tom is an engineering technician and still lives locally. Bob is currently working in Australia and Sam is a Royal Marine.

Butch was David Church's cousin and it was in 1987 that he started working with David in his agricultural engineering firm. Initially they worked locally but as the business evolved they travelled all over the UK, France, Corsica and Martinique. Another traveller!

In 1998 when David began to scale down the business Butch returned to sea again, fishing on 'Charlotte' and 'Prospector', both Southwold-based boats. At the same time he worked part time for Bodo, a friend of David's in his fabrication company out at Attleborough in Norfolk.

In 2002 Butch began working for Wally Webb, a local builder (funnily enough David Church was Best Man at Wally's wedding). Diane had just started running the Harbour Tea Rooms at Southwold so Butch had weekends free, this was when he first started helping on the ferry. He has been the regular 'Weekend Rower' ever since. In 2003 he was joined on the ferry by Digger his dog, and they make a great team. Butch is very popular with everyone, and children especially adore Digger.

Nick Beck

Nick was born in Poole, Dorset in 1967, and when he was four years old Nick's family moved to Topsham right beside the River Exe. It was on this very tidal river that he learnt to row and he was given his very own boat when he was just eight years old. It was a 12ft wooden clinker built dinghy, just a bit smaller than the ferry boat. He spent most of his spare time 'messing about on the river'.

He was a keen sailor and later became a sailing instructor in Salcombe for a couple of years when he left school. His first job was working for an architectural firm as their design librarian, but after the firm had mass redundancies in the 1980s he took a job as a freelance production manager for a theatre company in London, building and designing sets. This job involved travelling around Europe and even occasionally sent him worldwide.

In 1996 he decided a career change was a must so he enrolled on a boat building course at the International Boat Building School based in Oulton Broad, Suffolk and moved to Beccles. After his course finished he worked for Kingsley Farrington at Norwich, building traditional half decker sailing boats. In 1996 he changed jobs and went to work at Harbour Marine Services in Southwold. Nick first got involved with the ferry when he kindly offered to make a tiller for 'Oud Bob' for the Great River Race as the boat didn't have one. In 2005 Nick left Harbour Marine to set up his own boat repair and chandlery business in Beccles called Marine Service 50, but he decided to complement this by working one or two days a week on the ferry over the high summer months. He also rows competitively for Beccles rowing club. It seems he just can't get enough of boating!

Luke Jeans

Few people who cross the Blyth with the bearded ferryman Luke Jeans would suspect that he leads a double life. No, not as a secret agent but he has an equally exciting alter ego as a television director.

Luke was born in Walberswick many many years ago. His father at one point ran the Walberswick Pottery from East Point and along with Luke's grandfather ran Walberswick's only cinema during the war years. This may have sown the seeds in him for his future career path in film-making

After trying several schools, Luke ended up in London at the progressive school King Alfred's, which basically taught him that he liked drama. So, armed with one O'Level, he started work in the theatre, progressing from being stagehand to the youngest chief flyman in the country at that time, working the machinery for props, scenery, lighting etc – a highly responsible job.

Then he made the move into television, starting as a film editor with London Weekend TV and then on to directing and producing whilst also running a video editing company in Soho. Luke edited most of the first series of the *South Bank Show*, many pop promos and lots of documentaries. Directing credits are just as diverse, including the much-loved show *Blind Date*.

Luke enjoyed spending time back in Walberswick and as a keen fisherman he often stopped for a chat with ferryman David Church. He didn't suspect that he would one day be helping to provide the service himself. So why does he do that?

'Well it's a combination of fresh air, no stress, meeting a very diverse group of passengers, keeping a tradition alive and a complete change from television', which Luke still dabbles in during the winter months. In fact a lot of the passengers on the ferry say 'I think that you've got the best job in the world.' Well, Luke considers that he has two of the best jobs in the world (apart from wet Sunday mornings in March).

Chapter fourteen

Dani Church – my story

The first recollections I have of the ferry are sitting down at the hut with my Dad eating savoury cheesecakes laden with butter and sausage rolls that my Nanna Connie had made. It was quite a ritual that she or Auntie Hazel would bring Dad or Bob their morning refreshments. We often sat around the side of the hut as there it was sunny and out of the wind. There always seemed to be a lot of people around, mostly fisherman and locals who would sit chatting to my dad over their tartan thermos flasks of coffee. There seemed no hurry to life in those days, customers few and far between on those sunny mornings. It was such a great community; everyone seemed to me to be so happy.

When I was very young I loved to sit in the red and white life rings at the back of the boat listening to all the conversations, and stroking various dogs as dad rowed across. Dad disliked wearing shoes on the ferry in the summer months he would only wear his faded leather sandals he had made or just bare feet, always very tanned. He rarely wore a shirt in the summer time on the boat if it was warm I always loved the way the sun turned him brown so quickly. As he got older all that salt and sand creased his face accentuating those lovely laughter lines he had. I used to spend hours crab fishing on the ferry landing stage. As Dad knew lots of fisherman there was never a shortage of fish heads going, he taught me how to thread my crabbing line through the gills and out through the fish's mouth. Fish is great bait, bacon was unheard of as crabbing bait then, too much of a waste! I do recall falling or being pushed in the river a few times by a naughty boy who used to fish with me.

I don't remember exactly how old I was when Dad let me take to the oars, but I must have been around 6 or 7. Dad taught me to row by first making me sit opposite him and hold onto one oar with both hands. By doing this I had a feel for the motion of the oars without having to concentrate on much else. This progressed onto holding an oar in each hand opposite him and finally by sitting on his lap following what he did. There was one nasty incident when the oar got caught against the stage and I was pinned underneath the oar between Dad and the boat, I thought my back was going to snap but luckily the oar was freed off in time. When I finally rowed the boat on my own Dad would sit very close stepping in as soon as I fell prey to the tide and lost control of the boat. He was always incredibly patient, with whatever he was teaching me to do, never shouting at me. The ferry boat is a very heavy boat to row so I used to practice in the little fibreglass dinghy Dad had.

Below: a very early start – Dani at the oars with her sister Polly on board

I used to horse ride every weekend in Walberswick with my Auntie Hazel and I often used to hitch a lift over the river with Dad in the morning in that little dinghy when he went over to fetch the ferry boat which was always kept on the Walberswick side. Trips over in that dingy were always quite hazardous as it leaked and I would be positioned somewhere in the boat to balance it so the water wouldn't pour in too fast, my feet always up in the air as the bilges would be ankle deep in water. Part of the reason that boat leaked was because my friends and I had rowed it out the harbour mouth on a calm day but on a strong outgoing tide. Unable to row it in against the current we dragged the heavy hulk over the stones all the way back from the beach holing the bottom of it. Dad wasn't too pleased. A couple of times I had to leave the boat up the river towards Blythburgh when I had rowed up there with friends and couldn't make it back again against the tide. I often had to walk back the next day and row the boat back when the tide was going out again. Dad was always very trusting letting me do things like this; I suppose he knew it was all good experience to learn how strong that tide can be.

I must admit I do have a mild obsession with being down the river or on the beach. Maybe that's because many happy times were spent there in my childhood. Mum would take us to the beach most days in the summer and dad would take me out fishing for herring or sprats. Always up at the crack of dawn, he would be out there if the conditions were right, I never wanted to be there at 5 in the morning, in the freezing cold but once you were at sea and the sun was coming up and I would have a flask of hot chocolate and Dad with hip flask of sloe gin it all seemed worth it. Dad loved to make sloe gin and taught me his own special recipe. He taught me so many skills from cooking to even skinning a rabbit.

I loved steering the boat as he set or pulled in the nets, the herring glistening and still wriggling. I used to help get the fish out of the nets and one time when we were spratting, shaking the nets for the fish to fall out into the boat I suddenly passed out. I thought I was just sea sick but turns out I had been standing downwind of the exhaust pipe and had been overcome by fumes. I had to lay in the bottom of the boat with the fish until I felt better.

It must have been in my mid teens that Dad finally let me row the ferry boat over on my own. Firstly alone then he would let me take the odd passenger. He would sit on the ferry shed and watch. I'm sure very nervously, but he never let on. Everything had to be done properly. Oars put where they should be upon landing, boat kept clean, seats wiped, life rings kept in order, and all hands in the boat as you arrive at the landing stage. Really, I just watched Dad and copied how he did things. Dad was always very polite and welcoming to his customers, I hope I am like that too. It wasn't really until you are out on the river on your own that you really have to concentrate on what you are doing. I think the hardest thing when I first started was being able to talk to my customers and row at the same time.

There is quite an art to rowing the ferry as it is technique which gets you to the other side, not just strength. Dad taught me how to understand the wind and tide, using the sides of the river to row the boat up into, and then guiding it over in the strong tidal current in the middle. The river is about 18ft deep in the middle and only shallow at the sides so obviously the river runs much faster where it is deepest. I was very nervous taking my first passengers across, although everyone was always very nice.

I was born in 1973 and grew up in Keens Lane, Reydon. I went to school locally, Reydon Infants, Southwold Primary, then to Reydon High School. For me, Reydon High was a great school because it was so small. Everyone knew each other and each others families too. I could bike to school and it finished at 2.45pm so there was plenty of time for activities afterwards. I made some very good friends there which I still have, and am lucky that most people who I went to school with still live around here, I think this is really important in a community. I loved school but was never one for being inside for too long and remember yearning to be outside not stuck in the classroom. I really wanted to be a vet when I was at school but didn't get good enough grades at GCSE so went on to do French, Biology and Chemistry A levels at Sir John Leman High School at Beccles.

I changed my mind about my career and decided to follow conservation as I hoped it would mean I would be able to work outside. I then did a degree at York University in Ecology Conservation and the Environment. It was a great three years of my life but unlike most of my fellow students as soon as holiday time came I was straight back home as I missed it immensely and I would work back at home for mum in her shop 'The Quayhole' down by the river or behind the bar in The Bell Inn. I didn't really have much to do with the ferry at this time, I suppose other things were more interesting, such as friends and beach parties, but I do remember taking my Dad many caramel slices and ice creams whilst he was working, he did have a sweet tooth, and having the odd row now and again.

At University I was lucky enough to do my third year project in Egypt, studying fish on coral reefs. In 1993 I and two other girls were allowed to camp in the Marine National Park near Sharm el Sheik for the summer. It was amazing. After this adventure the thrill of travelling ate into me and I longed to go to travel more. I always felt I should also be working though so after graduating went to live in North Wales and worked voluntarily for CEFAS studying lobster burrowing behaviour. This luckily helped me get a temporary job at the CEFAS laboratory in Lowestoft so I could come back home. However it was then that my old tutor from college contacted me and said that I if I wanted he knew of an educational conservation school out in the bush in Zimbabwe that I could go and help at for six weeks. I jumped at the chance and disappeared off there on my own over Easter 1996. It was such an experience, elephants walking past your camp at night and endless snakes in the bath. I had time to travel about in Zimbabwe for a bit too, which was eye opening. The time went quickly and I was soon back at CEFAS at the job they had kindly kept open for me but by that December I had given that job up and gone travelling around Thailand for 6 months. Mum and Dad always encouraged me to travel.

It was when I returned from Thailand, jobless that Dad suggested I should go on the course to do my Boat Masters Licence which would mean that I could officially help him on the ferry. I successfully did this and it was then that I started to help him on the very odd occasion. Sometimes I would cover the lunch break for him, if it was busy and on bank holidays and crabbing Sunday I would row the old ferry boat whilst he rowed the new one he had so proudly just had built. It is always fun doing two boats on the ferry as the pressure is off a bit as you can clear the queues much quicker and have time for a quick cup of tea. Of course the ferry is only seasonal so I really felt I should have a 'proper' job too. I managed to be taken on as an Environment Protection Assistant for the Environment Agency. I remember my Boss saying that he had seen in my 'other interest' section on the application form I had written that I helped row the ferry and he was intrigued (I do wonder if that's how I got the interview). I worked full time for the Environment Agency based in Norwich from 1997 until 2001 when I went part time as I had intended to help Dad on the ferry as he had been ill and wanted to take a step back.

Below: Dani with her dog, Nellie

Unfortunately this never happened as strangely enough and so sadly Dad died the day I had chosen to work part time from. He knew and was relieved that I intended to keep the ferry running. I was honoured that he trusted me to carry on his business. Its funny, but all the time I was at University and working I always knew that one day I would be the ferryman, so never really took my career that seriously. I just never envisaged that I would be running the ferry so early on in my life, I do wish that I had helped Dad more when he was rowing, but I never knew that he would not be around to do it with me later, I always thought we would be a team together. I left the Environment Agency the following year, I couldn't manage a part time job whilst running a business as well. I learnt a lot from my time there and was sad to leave but it was the best thing to do.

So now it was up to me to make sure that the ferry ran
smoothly. It was extremely overwhelming everything that had to be
done. Luckily Geoff Ryder who was helping Dad out when he was
ill continued to do a lot of the rowing that first year so I had much
help. Geoff and Daisy his dog became a well known pair on the river
that year. Daisy had a tendency to jump off the boat and swim across
the river, worrying many of the customers, who were relieved she
made it each time, even when she got back in the boat and shook all
over them... There is so much to do keeping the ferry running
smoothly. Firstly manning it is difficult, providing a reliable service
is important if you want to ensure people keep using it which means
someone has to be on duty whenever we say we will be open. There
is no chance of calling in sick, as there is no one to call into. Having
said that, outdoors definitely reduces the risk of all the colds etc you
get from being enclosed in air conditioned offices with lots of
people.

The landing stages have to be properly maintained so people don't slip over which means lots of creosoting to stop mud and algae building up. Both landing stages have had to be replaced in the last 2 years at great expense. The constant wear and tear of boats knocking against them, strong tides and crazy customers who rock the pontoons and hang off the posts all takes it toll. The boats have to be taken out of the water (too heavy a task for me alone) then scrubbed rubbed down and repainted each year, ready for inspection for their licences. The health and safety and admin side of things all takes time. However, my enjoyment of the rowing and love of the job make up for all this.

Since I have been doing the ferry I have met many interesting people and made lots of new friends. There was one summer in particular I made a note of which countries abroad people were coming from. I had people crossing from Canada, New Zealand, Kenya, Hong Kong, Mexico, South Africa Gambia, Sweden, Holland, America, Australia, France, Germany and Japan. The man from Kenya had never seen the sea before that day. The man from Japan must be my most interesting customer to date. He was cycling round Britain from lighthouse to lighthouse, he hardly spoke a word of English.

Most of my ferry customers are lovely and like to share their stories. I went to New Zealand in 2003 and brought a TUI (NZ beer) cap over there which I used to wear on the ferry. Some New Zealanders spotted it when they were coming over a couple of years later and it sparked off conversation. Only a few weeks later a parcel arrived for me in the post addressed to the ferry girl, Walberswick. They had sent me a new cap as they thought the other was looking so tatty. I often receive photos and cards from my customers which is really lovely of them. In the 7 years I have been doing the ferry it has been great to watch all the children who regularly come over grow up and listen to the stories of what they have been up to.

Other interesting customers have included a mouse which was caught by a friend staying in one of the huts down by the river, he couldn't bear to kill it so made me set it free on the opposite side of the river. A local man has been known to come down and sit on the ferry playing his mandolin to unsuspecting customers. An elderly lady who sang me the wonderful few lines of the song 'row me over the river do boatman do' I was so taken with this little tune that I wrote down the words and my friend Thea put them onto a plaque which sits proudly on the ferry hut.

An Opera singer serenaded me throughout the whole journey once. I've had various dogs of all shapes and sizes, and pieces of furniture coming back from the local antiques shop Tinkers. Along with the numerous gulls that perch on the jetty there was also once a snake wrapped around the ferry post waiting one morning when I arrived, I never fancied taking him across. Three tandems and six people in one trip was quite a squeeze and quite a few wind/kite surfers who have been blown from one beach to another and need to get back to their cars (they never have any money these ones!). I mustn't forget all the local celebrities who come over from time to time. There is a quote in a book called *Siddhartha* by Herman Hesse which says, 'the ferryman has to go nowhere as everyone comes to him'. This is so very true.

In 2004 a ferry customer had mentioned to my colleague Butch about a race he thought we should enter on the River Thames called the Great River Race. We looked into it and found out that it is a 22 mile charity race from Ham near Richmond to Greenwich for traditional rowed craft, taking place in the September. I, Crispin Butch and his wife Diane trained that summer, then took part in the race. It was amazing. It was the first time the boat 'Oud Bob' had left the river Blyth, we towed the boat on a trailer someone lent us, all the way to London behind our transit van.

Rowing up the Thames was very bizarre, especially going past the Houses of Parliament. Many of our ferry customers had turned out to watch us and there was a lot of cheering from some of the bridges as we rowed under. A mini bus was organised from Walberswick so that friends and family could come up and watch. They sailed up and down the Thames on a pleasure boat, calling words of encouragement as they passed us. It was truly a wonderful experience. Rowing under Tower Bridge was quite hair raising as the tide and pleasure boats were causing a big swell there, but we made the finish line easily coming 82nd out of nearly three hundred boats, Oud Bob did us proud. The fact that we had raised £3890 mostly from the generosity of my ferry customers, for The Sandra Chapman Unit at James Paget Hospital where my Dad had received fantastic care when he was ill, made the whole thing really worthwhile.

Below: a long way from home – the team in Oud Bob (bottom right)

*More scenes from The Great River Race – facing page Oud Bob (bottom right)
seems tiny on the River Thames*

Whilst doing this race we met a rowing coach from Cambridge, Don Hefferon who kindly took us under his wing and gave us many valuable tips. He kindly arranged for us to attend Henley Regatta with him and a friend, Martin Fordham and then organised for a group from Southwold to go and try 'proper' rowing at Trinity College Boathouse. They gave up their time and had us all rowing up and down the Cam on one lovely warm summer's day in 2005. It was a memory I will always treasure. I have been given all these fantastic opportunities just from being on the ferry.

So what do I enjoy about my job? I love being in the fresh air and never having to be inside. The peace and quiet of the river first thing in the morning and late afternoon, when most people have gone home. Having time to watch the river, the birds, the seal and the weather. Having time to read a book or a quick nap in the boat on quiet days. The challenge of the rowing and knowing you are keeping a tradition alive. It would be all too easy to use a motor boat all the time, although I couldn't stand the smell of fuel and the noise. Its the exercise and the fact that I can eat what I like during the summer months as you burn it off so quickly which I love.

Dad always had a fried breakfast before he rowed on a Saturday, I can still remember the smell of the bacon and mushrooms in the kitchen; he couldn't stand eating salad after a day on the ferry. After a days rowing you feel you can enjoy a good meal and a beer and know you have earned it. It's great, meeting new people and watching my regular customers and children who come on the boat and seeing how much they enjoy the crossing, finding out what has been happening in their lives year after year.

Many people just love to sit and watch the ferry, as it's such a novelty. Some people sit in their cars day after day just watching and enjoying it. It's comforting sometimes to know people are looking out for you in case there is a problem. Its funny peoples reactions to me when they see that I am a girl not a big strapping man. Many comments such as 'are you sure you can make it' or; I feel guilty you doing the rowing and not one of the men on the boats', and 'lets feel your muscles'. I had a son Charlie in 2007 and many people comment that it's a good job he's a boy so he can help you when he gets older! What's wrong with a girl doing it I wonder?

Once while on holiday with Crispin in Morocco, we went to go on a ferry boat to a nearby beach and I offered to row - the guy, slightly taken aback, agreed, I think he thought it was a joke, but I rowed the boat the whole distance to the beach. It was about four times as far as our usual ferry journey across the River Blyth, and a bit harder than I thought but I was determined to get there and I made it, and we had quite a laugh with the boys (they didn't offer me a job though!)

Below: a 'busman's holiday'? Dani rowing the ferry boat in Morocco

*Opposite and left: Charlie
on board the ferry boat*

*Below: Hazel delivers a
welcome flask of tea*

150

I don't like mobile phones ringing or being used on the boat as it spoils the whole atmosphere of the crossing for everybody on board. It's also difficult on really busy days, then you end up feeling like a machine and not a ferryman at all, sometimes you feel your arms and back will never make another crossing. Most people are happy to queue though as long as the weather is fine, waiting on the landing stage is part of the fun anyway.

Auntie Hazel always makes these days more bearable as she struggles past the queue with her cup of tea she brings for me twice a day, every day I am rowing. I am so pleased to see that tea on some days; she is so kind hearted. The commitment of the business is very hard, but in the last few years I have got a really good team of ferryman behind me, there are five of us all together now. Adrian (Butch) Church who is my Dads cousin, and Crispin my boyfriend have been a fantastic help since 2002.

Above: Dani and Crispin share the work of rowing

Luke Jeans and Nick Beck both started helping in 2005, without these people's dedicated help I would be struggling to keep the ferry going. Crispin and I decided to start a family in 2007 and rowing whilst pregnant or with a baby is not easy, in fact almost impossible, especially now that our son Charlie is a toddler and very mobile. I only row three days a week now and that's enough at the moment.

The future of the ferry is obviously very important to me. I have concerns about the number of costs and regulations that we now have to meet, although I do of course appreciate the need for health and safety. Currently, we have to comply with the following:

Boat and public liability insurances x 3
Employer's liability insurance

Boat Licences
Ferry Licence
Ferry stage rent
Harbour dues
Hut rents
Boat upkeep/ repaints
Jetty maintenance/ replacement
Boat engine servicing
Boat Inspections
Lifejacket safety Checks
Flares
Life rings
Boatmasters licences
First aid course
Fire extinguisher checks/ replacement
Electric outboard
VHF radio and operators licence.

The uncertainty about coastal flooding in this area and the instability of the harbour wall is worrying as it is unsure how quickly this will impact on the river and surrounding area. It is already noticeable the changes in tidal speed and the impact on the river banks. When the whole structure of the river eventually changes I hope that the ferry service will be able to gradually adapt accordingly as it has done over the past 800 years. It would be good to think that the ferry will continue within our family, but nothing is ever certain. My Dad told me to keep the ferry going for as long as I enjoy it, so that's what I plan to do.

Chapter fifteen

Ferry Dogs

Over the years, many of the ferrymen have had a constant companion while rowing back and forth across the river. It seems only right to pay tribute to those important characters of the past and present – the ferry dogs.

Sitting comfortably? Bonnie and her master Young Bob Cross

Above: Jinx   Right: Trixie
Below: Young Bob with Bonnie

Old Bob with Rusty

Young Bob with Cassie

Above: Old Bob with Rusty, Bruce and Ruffles

Right: Bonnie

Above: Young Bob and Bonnie

Right: Digger

Above: Polly's dog, Marley
Below: Geoff and Daisy

Dani's dog, Nellie

Chapter sixteen

Miscellaneous Memories of the Ferry Service

Arthur Brown, Ferryman

Arthur was born in Wangford in 1890, and as a young boy he was both strong-willed and resourceful: he used to keep a pipe and tobacco hidden in a tree near his home, and when his mother sent him shopping he would tell her that the price of groceries had gone up – he had spent the extra on tobacco.

At the age of 15 he joined up with the Navy and worked on destroyers, and later he married Elizabeth Hurr, the daughter of a local fisherman. Towards the end of the Second World War Arthur, by then in his fifties, came out of the Navy and began working on the ferry with Frank Palmer. He was living in Southwold at Coastguard Row, number 21 Victoria Street, and his wages were £2 10 shillings a week. The money was paid via Harrissons the solicitors, as Leonard Harrisson was then secretary of the River Blyth Ferry Company, his employer.

When talking about those days Arthur would add that at that time a pint of beer cost 10 old pence, just under a shilling, so he couldn't afford too many pints each week. To help the household finances, his wife made some money by being a mannequin for dresses and suits, she was very tall and slim, and she also worked for Mr Critten the Mayor.

Some of Arthur's customers were generous with tips, and at Christmas the greengrocers who used to bring their produce across on the ferry would throw fruit to him as a present. This extra bonus was welcome, except that on one occasion an orange hit him and broke his pocket watch.

Arthur's daughter Betty Jinks remembers that when the dancer Santos Cosini came across on the ferry, he danced on top of his car as it went across. Like all of the ferrymen, Arthur had many stories to tell, but then, so did his customers. The postman's daughter, Madge Beane, nee Welton, commented that Arthur Brown was the only man who ever made her mother blush; 'some would say that he was little saucy,' she says.

He enjoyed his work, and people say he always looked healthy: he had a ruddy complexion and his hair never went grey. In character he was quite stern but very helpful - Betty Jinks remembers him as a wonderful father. He gave up his job on the ferry when the pontoon was put out of service, and he wasn't inclined to operate the rowing boat.

In later life Arthur worked in the British Legion and then eventually he became the landlord of the Old Royal pub in Victoria Street, Southwold, which he managed until his retirement. When he finished at the pub he lived on the seafront, but he suffered from bad bronchitis in his later years. Arthur died in 1964 at the age of 74.

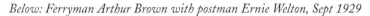

Below: Ferryman Arthur Brown with postman Ernie Welton, Sept 1929

Robert English – man of many trades

Robert English rowed the ferry for only a few years from roughly 1944–1947 but he certainly made an impression on his customers. He was renowned for being a man of little patience who could be incredibly awkward if he felt like it, but was however a reliable ferryman who helped out Old Bob Cross or Ernie when they needed him.

Robert English, also known as Bob, was born in Walberswick and was the grandson of the former ferryman Robert English who worked with Todd at the end of the 18th century. Born in 1888 in Walberswick, he was the second son of George English and Mary May (she was the sister of Sam May, one time cox of Southwold lifeboat). He joined the Navy as a stoker in 1906, and in 1916 he took part in the Battle of Jutland, the largest sea battle of World War One and considered in some aspects to have been the largest naval battle in history.

Below: Robert English helps two young cyclists off the rowing ferry along the narrow, slippery jetty. Note in the background the chain ferry The Blyth lies abandoned.

Bob married Ada Chaplin in 1917 and left the Navy in 1919, remaining on the reserve list. The couple had four sons: Ron, George, Owen and Anthony and a daughter named Peggy. He was a dedicated family man.

After the Navy, he made a living as a long shore fisherman and he was also the swimming instructor for the village, but his method of teaching was not popular and even his son Ron never learnt to swim as his teaching technique scared him so much.

Bob could be quite cantankerous, as former Walberswick postmaster Arthur Sharman remembers. Arthur used to live in Southwold, and both he and his sister had to cross the river to get to work in Walberswick. He says, 'We'd call Bob English to come and pick us up and sometimes he would be awkward and not come over. We'd be up to our knees in mud trying to get into another boat, and he would say we weren't allowed to do that, as he was the only one authorised to take people across.'

Madge Beane broke this rule one day. She recalls that Bob often used to take an early lunch when he felt like it, and often on Wednesdays when she only had to work half day in Walberswick so then she had a long wait to get across the river to go home to Southwold. One day this had happened and she found the local baker also stranded, so they hijacked the rowing boat and Madge, having watched the ferryman and learned about tackling the tide, made the amazing effort and rowed them across. No doubt there was a big fuss when Bob found his boat had gone!

Although he was a tough swimming teacher, his own skill was invaluable as he saved the life of a local boy who had drifted out to sea in a small boat. Although it was a kind-hearted rescue, he was so angry with the lad that he lost his temper and punished him severely for which he received a fine from the police. This money was however reimbursed to him by a villager, as although he had behaved badly he had been brave too.

Robert's fishing career was cut short by the second war and he turned his hand to many things: handyman, general labourer and ferryman too. He lived out his years in Beach View, opposite Fishers garage in Walberswick, and died in 1968 at the age of 80.

Arthur Sharman – post master at Walberswick 1945 -1986

Arthur's father ran the Post Office from 1933 to 1943, when Ernie Welton was the postman. Arthur had to cycle to school at Reydon Area Council School. They were issued cycles and given vouchers from the school printed on yellow paper which stated a free trip for him and his cycle on the ferry. He had to get to school by 8 am. Arthur Brown and Frank Palmer were working on the ferry then. 'You had to be good around Arthur Brown as he didn't trust children on the boat,' says Mr Sharman.

He remembers being on the chain ferry when they spotted a man swimming up the river. The engine roared and the pontoon started going across, and the man came at it fast as the tide was in full spate. Everyone was shouting at him to be careful but he swam straight into the ferry and hit his head on the pontoon. Strangely enough he just swam off again and nobody knew who he was.

As well as the post and various groceries, a coal lorry used to cross on the chain ferry and Arthur says when the tide was low the metal ramps were steep and slippery, causing the truck to struggle to get off. Arthur remembers the sad fate of The Blyth; 'After the war the chain ferry hung in the middle of the river so no one could get to it, it was sinking on one side,' he says.

The Blyth, having sunk on a previous occasion when a chain broke

When he ran the Post Office from 1945 to 86 the mail was brought across the river, it was a very reliable service and he says that nothing untoward ever happened to it. If the Post Office in Southwold was short staffed he would go on the ferry and help by collecting the mail from them. Unfortunately one day when he was carrying all the mail he lost his balance and stepped off the boat the wrong side into the mud. Ferryman Bob Cross quickly helped him out and by a miracle all the post was intact.

When Arthur was in the Post Office he always remembered Seymore Lucas the artist coming in and saying, 'Sharman, those sh***ing little old geese of Bob Cross's have messed all over my shoes.' Arthur couldn't help laughing.

George Balls, Electrical Engineer

George was born in 1924 and he started working for the Southwold electrical firm East Anglian Supply Company in 1938. The company owned a two wheels hand pushed metal truck, which they loaded up with electrical gear, and this might even include cookers for installation or repair work at Walberswick He would push this down the road and have to cross over on the ferry. George said he didn't like low tide as the jetty was 'right slippery' then, and it was difficult to get the heavy trolley onto the pontoon. Unfortunately the ferrymen didn't offer to help him with his task, and so he was very relieved when the company eventually got a van and he could drive round, even though it was a much longer journey by road.

After the war George worked for Billy Denny the builder, and he said that all the labourers would pile into the rowing boat, five men and five cycles. He recalled that it cost about tuppence (2d) then. They were always scared to get off the boat at the other side because the ferry geese would chase them. 'They won't hurt you boy' Old Bob would say as they came towards you, wings flapping out. But the men would be quick to get on their bikes and cycle away.

Madge Beane nee Welton

Madge's father Ernie Welton was the much-loved postman in Walberswick for 17 years until 1941. He lived in Southwold and used the ferry six times a day, three times each way.

During the war, just before her father retired, Madge began using the ferry regularly too. She went to work at Reynolds grocery shop, covering for the men who were away fighting, including her intended fiancé Peter Reynolds. Sadly her loved one was killed in the war.

Ernie Welton (top right) on the ferry

Among her many memories are the Scottish herring girls who used to come to Southwold for the season, and they would knit as they walked down to the ferry. Madge clearly remembers their big, brawny arms.

The chain ferry had all kinds of problems in its last few years, and when tides were low the cobbled slipway would be green and slippery, so two planks of wood had to be put down to offer some grip. Car drivers would have to rev their engines and make a dash onto the pontoon or risk slithering and not making it.

Occasionally a chain would be broken or the tide would be too strong, and then if possible a rowing boat would be used instead. The small but strong former boxer Frank Palmer was ferryman then, and could usually get his passengers across.

Frank came to Madge's aid many a time, such as when the tide was so high the jetty was under water. Frank gave her a piggyback to get to the boat, and took her across. Another time they both arrived at the jetty and found the boat had gone: they walked along the shore and found it by the Harbour Inn, stuck fast in the mud. Frank had to lever it out with an iron bar before he could start the journey.

Sometimes when boats went missing the culprits were the troops who were stationed in the area. Soldiers would borrow a boat but not tie it up afterwards and it would be left to drift away. Madge also remembers seeing piles of clothes on the shore, as soldiers swam across the river, then she would see white bodies running up the road. One wonders where they might have been going like that.

Bob and Ernie Cross were the next ferrymen to operate the service and Madge liked Bob best of all. She felt sorry for him when she saw his hands looking so sore and weather-beaten. He was out in all conditions, but one winter's day he couldn't row the boat across to fetch her as there were ice sheets floating down the river from Blythburgh. He managed to throw a rope across and she, with the local baker who was also stranded there, hauled the boat over, then Bob pulled it back to the other side. The service was then suspended and Madge had to spend three nights at the shop with no other means of getting home except a very long walk round.

The ferry was stuck on another occasion when the tide was so low that there wasn't enough water in the river to row across. Customers were relieved when a bridge was finally built.

Madge finished working at Reynolds in 1945 at Christmas. She had been crossing the river for four and a half years, and she was so sad not to be using the ferry again with Old Bob at the oars, that she couldn't bring herself to say goodbye to him, and walked away from the boat without telling him it was her last trip.

Richard Fisk, Postman

Richard worked for the Post Office from 1947 to 1992. During his early days as a postman one of his delivery routes was over the River Blyth to Walberswick, always by bicycle.

He said, 'When the weather was good we cycled down to the harbour with a waterproof bag full of parcels, packets and bundles of letters, plus our waterproofs on the front carrier. Also across one shoulder we had our delivery pouch containing more letters and packets delivering to the Golf Club and Harbour Cottages, on the way to the ferry. We then put our cycle, still loaded up, into the rowing boat, and the Ferryman – either Old Bob or Ernie Cross – would row us over the river. Four trips a day, two each way. It's funny we always called the ferrymen Bob or Ernie, everyone else was Mr or Mrs.'

Old Bob Cross helps Richard Fisk on the ferry with his heavy load

'When I was on the round, the ferry ran all year, weather permitting. If the Office phone rang about 6.30 am while we were preparing our deliveries and the shout went up: NO FERRY we knew the weather was too rough for the ferry to run. We then had to cycle over the common to the old railway track and over the Bailey bridge, head down against strong winds, rain or snow - it was always easier when the ferry was running.'

Richard was junior postman for a while and one of his jobs was to ride the post office tricycle down to the ferry, full of the Walberswick parcels that the other postman couldn't carry on his bike. He would give them to Bob or Ernie, who would row them across and keep an eye on them in the hut until the postman had finished his delivery and could fit them on his bicycle. Old Bob was not always pleased to see the postman and Richard remembers Bob often pretending to be busy in the boat and ignoring him so he would have to shout over to get his attention.

Bob was a gruff fellow, but not a grumpy old boy, and his customers felt concern for him. 'The tides are so strong on the river and I always hoped Old Bob would keep rowing, because he was an old boy, I used to think I hope you don't collapse,' said Richard.

One day the other postman, Brian Burrage, saw Bob asleep in the boat and thought he would surprise him by creeping up on him. Unfortunately his load that day was wide and heavy and he slipped, the bicycle went in, post and all. No doubt Bob woke up pretty sharpish at that.

When the ferry service later ran only in the summer months, the post was less frequently taken on the boat, and more often cycled over the bridge. When postal vans were introduced onto the round in 1989, this marked the end of an era for the postmen on bicycles in Walberswick.

Former postman Richard Fisk with ferrywoman
Dani Church, October 2004

Philip Kett, Errand Boy

Philip says, 'The year was 1949 and I was in my last year at Walberswick County Primary School before moving on to Reydon Secondary Modern aged eleven. On Monday mornings I had the job of being errand boy, this was after roll call and the register had been signed. My duty was to collect the meat for the week and deliver it to Mrs Stannard who cooked our school dinners in her own home, this was done in her two-burner paraffin oil oven and on top of oil stoves, catering for about twenty of us children.'

'So every Monday morning I would collect the string bag from Mrs Stannard and take myself off to the ferry to wait for Norman's butchers van to deliver the meat to the ferry. In summer time when the weather was nice I would explore the boats that were pulled up on the shore and anything else that took my fancy, but when the weather was rough I was allowed to sit in the ferryman's hut, which at that time was a corrugated iron shed with no windows in it save for a small piece of glass embedded in the door at exactly the right height for Old Bob or Ernie to see out. They could see both of the ferry stages from there whilst sitting on the wooden bench inside the hut, although most days the door would be open if the weather was reasonable.'

'The interior of the hut was an Aladdin's cave of trinkets: bits and bobs relating to the ferry and fishing, net needles of all sizes, some made of wood, some made of bone. Also shackles, twine, chain, spare rowlocks, fish hooks, in fact all manner of odds and ends.'

'By 1949 the Bailey bridge had been put across the river on the supports of the closed Southwold Railway, and the ferry trade was much reduced.'

Frank Reed: celebrating life

These two snaps were provided by Frank Reed of Stowmarket who, in 1947, took a celebratory cycle ride with his friend Jim Payne, in gratitude for their having survived the war. Frank still remembers that the ferry played a part in their trip, for which they paid a penny each for the ride, and extra for their bikes.

Above: Jim Payne
Left: Frank Reed

Dr Andrew and Mrs Alice Eastaugh : celebrating marriage

Ferryman Luke Jeans was delighted to put on his dinner jacket to take Dr and Mrs Eastaugh for a sunset ride to celebrate their silver wedding anniversary in September 2007.

Vida Connick

Vida can still recall the sounds of the pontoon ferry, from its shrill whistle to the creaking and groaning of the chains. The little engine shed was very noisy, she says.

Her uncle, Robert Hood Spall, used to own the Wavecrest Tearooms, famed for delicious ice cream, and the ice needed for making it was brought across on the old ferry. The tearoom was down by the ferry at Walberswick, it was a wooden building on stilts, and it was washed away down the river in the 1953 floods.

During the war, the villagers of Walberswick used to grow as much home produce as they could, and every week they would donate baskets of vegetables to be sent to seamen on the minesweepers, so Vida had the job of taking it down to the ferry. She always managed that without mishap, but one day when she had her bike loaded with a basket of shopping there was a problem as Bob Cross was getting it out of the boat and the bicycle tipped over, spilling her sausages into the river where they were carried away by the tide.

Vida knew several of the ferrymen including Ernie, 'Old Bob' and 'Young Bob' Cross. She comments, 'In those days we didn't call people by their Christian names, we had a lot more respect, and so I called them all Mr Cross.'

Below: Vida with David Church

In November 1944 Vida and her husband were expecting their first baby, but Richard was away on war work in London repairing bomb-damaged properties. She went into labour but needed to pop across to Southwold for supplies to take into Halesworth hospital with her. As she tried to get into the ferry boat Ernie Cross the ferryman said 'Are you trying to sink my bloody boat?!' She promised him that she wasn't.

For a time the local council closed the Bailey bridge for repair, and provided a temporary ferry service in addition to the one being run by Old Bob Cross. In the photograph above, Vida is seen waiting to board as ferryman Derek Allen, (centre) helps to put a bike on the boat.

Chris Coleman: David Church's Fellow Ferryman

Chris first visited Walberswick when he was nine years old, when his family decided to come on holiday from London to a house at Moorside on Walberswick common. The house they stayed in was owned by Mrs Cathy Fisher. Cathy was a great friend of Connie Church, Old Bob's daughter and because of this Chris was introduced to her son David Church as they were the same age. Chris and David became instant friends.

David's love of the ferry was contagious, so it wasn't long before Chris found himself down the river, getting the hang of rowing. Chris's family continued to visit Walberswick for their holidays and Chris would follow, but he often would travel down alone and spend a week staying at Ocean View with David. In 1956 Chris started spending the whole of his school holidays in Walberswick and he and David would work the ferry to help out Old Bob.

Chris Coleman at the oars

Chris recalls, 'In 1958 we had a fantastic week and made £25 on the ferry. That was an immense sum of money in those days; the fare was only two old pence per person then. David and I always shared the money between us, and paid some over to Bob. Old Bob Cross was getting old then so we only opened the ferry at Easter, school holidays and a bit of time in June and September.'

They did more than simply operating the ferry service: Young Bob and Boco English would get David and Chris to row them out to sea in the ferry boat to go herring fishing and seine netting. Seine netting is a way of catching sea trout: the net would be fixed at one end and they would row the boat around it. David and Chris rowed a set of oars each whilst Bob and Boco sat and drank their beers. 'It was a wonderful experience,' says Chris.

So from the mid 1950s to early 1960s Chris and David rowed together. 'We never fell out, as we always fancied different women and there were plenty of girls about. No one ever fell in apart from a few people we didn't like,' he jokes.

'David and I both think we saw the ferry ghost. Looking across one day there was a man waiting for the ferry but as we rowed over to get him he disappeared. It's very open down the river so you can see people coming and going, but this man just vanished...'

Chris went off to study geography, geology and philosophy at Aberystwyth University and then on to Oxford for a degree in Social Administration. His life gradually moved back to London as he became a banker. He would still however take weeks off to come down and help on the ferry and spend time in Walberswick. Later after David married and had children, Chris would stand in so David could take a holiday with his family. Chris finally moved to Walberswick in the late 1980s and now runs a lampshade company based in Halesworth. He remained friends with David until the end. 'I miss him,' he says.

Letters to the Editor

Over the years, many people have written to their local newspaper when an article or photo involving the ferry has evoked fond memories.

In the East Anglian Magazine of October 1962 **Mr S F Watson** of Westerfield near Ipswich said of the chain ferry, 'In its later years the pontoon developed a tendency to settle down in mid stream. It is a pity that it could not be preserved as a museum piece.'

Christopher Elliott of Wimbledon wrote to the *East Anglian Daily Times* in 2001, saying that before the war he had used the chain ferry until its demise, and he wondered if anyone had saved the name plate from it. No-one knows the answer. Mr Elliott described the ferrymen's hut as 'really a little museum of seashore relics,' which paints a charming picture. He added, 'Certainly the ferrymen, at different times, gave me coins and, found at Benacre, a fine seaman's medallion inscribed *St Paul – Pray For Us.*'

The Blyth – did the name plate survive?

Photos by Christopher Elliott

Top: the enchanting hut
Bottom: the loaded ferry boat approaches the jetty while in the background the chain ferry The Blyth lies derelict

Mr C E B Thompson of Woodbridge stated that he had been a Second Lieutenant in the Royal Engineers during the war, and in the summer of 1940 he was involved in laying mines along the coast between Kessingland and Southwold. He also blocked Southwold Harbour with two wooden hulks, but the strong tides broke them up within days. The soldiers used the chain ferry, but Mr Thompson remembers that the ferryman became angry because they didn't pay. This was probably Frank Palmer, because on one occasion he refused to allow the General to cross in his car until the fare was paid.

In a personal letter to the author, **Mrs Margaret Chadd MBE, nee Collett**, recalled that she and her father used to take their horses on the ferry during the 1930s, they would have a wonderful early morning ride over the bracken and gorse at Walberswick and then go back across the ferry to return home for breakfast.

Doris Mackley of Brooke near Norwich says she also took horses across the river on the ferry, from St Felix School in Southwold where she was a pupil in the 1930s.

Elephants and ghosts

One topic guaranteed to bring about a flood of memories and anecdotes is the tale of two circus elephants which may, or may not, have been taken across the River Blyth on the ferry. There are so many people who insist that they saw this happen, that it must surely be true, but no hard evidence in the form of a news report or photos has yet been found. An alternative version says that the elephants, apparently from Bronco Bill's Circus and named Sultan and Saucy, refused to cross and were taken round by road. Here is a selection of viewpoints.

In 1988 **Mrs G Lockwood** of Thorndon near Eye wrote that her mother's friend saw the incident: 'A circus was travelling between Southwold and Halesworth. Apparently the elephant keeper got separated from the main caravan. He took the wrong turning and ended up at the ferry with his two elephants.'

'The ferryman got the elephants on the ferry but found their weight was too much. He told the keeper that he would have to take one at a time, but the elephants decided otherwise. They refused to be separated in spite of persuasion by their keeper, who at last decided to retrace his steps back to the correct road.'

Also in that year **Harold Cross**, son of ferryman Wessy, insisted, 'The Walberswick school children were taken down to the river Blyth to see (the elephants). The ferry at that time was smaller than the later one, and was limited to what weight it could carry. When moving the elephants they travelled where possible on the roads, where they could feed on the way.'

He ended, 'I am now in my 87th year and one of my family had a photo of the event, but over the years it has been lost.'

The pontoon was replaced in 1927 and Weston Cross was indeed ferryman at that time. An unnamed contributor to the Women's Institute book *Suffolk Within Living Memory*, also seems to put the event in the 1920s. She too says the Walberswick children were let out of school to go and see the elephants cross the river, although they would only go on to the ferry one at a time.

In *Country Life* magazine the elephant issue arose in correspondence starting in January 1981 when **Colin Forsyth** of London wrote to say that he had been reliably informed that the pre-war steam ferry was 'finally sunk' by the weight of a cow elephant and its calf. Mr Forsyth reported that apparently the mother had refused to be parted from her calf and this led to the 'gross overloading of the ferry.' He expressed an interest in hearing from others who might know about the story.

In response, **Sam Curtis** of Hampshire agreed that he had heard the story that the ferry had been sunk by elephants. In the March edition he wrote, 'The ferry had a tariff of fares which ended with "All other animals 1d", and when a circus wanted to cross the river, the ferryman did not know what to charge for the elephants – I think there were three of them – as they were not listed on the tariff. He asked a clergyman sitting sketching on the river bank what he should charge. The answer was that the elephants came under the heading "All other animals". Mr Curtis concludes that it was the weight of the three elephants that sank the ferry.

In a letter to the *East Anglian Daily Times* in 2008. **Derek Johnson** of Reydon mentions that an elderly resident told him that an elephant had once crossed on the ferry.

Hazel Church also says that her grandfather, the ferryman 'Old' Bob Cross, had told her about the event, for he said that he was the one who had taken both elephants across, adding 'not a breath was drawn until we reached the other side.'

Below: the circus passes through Halesworth – but did the elephants ever cross the River Blyth on the Southwold-Walberswick Ferry?

Finally, **Madge Beane** says she remembers that it did happen in the mid 1920s; the elephants refused to cross together on the ferry so the trainer tried to make them wade across but he was worried that they might cut their feet if there was debris on the river bed. Nevertheless, Madge says that they braved it and reached the other side after lots of chin-wading, and with trunks held high.

As a postscript, A. Barrett Jenkins recalled that in the early 1900s performing Russian bears were brought to Southwold but when it came to crossing the river, the trainer refused to pay for a ferry passage for the animals and so he made the bears swim across.

The other subject which is most likely to provoke a spate of stories, is that of ghosts. As mentioned in chapter two, ferryman George Todd was apparently well acquainted with his spectral customers – or at least, he simply noticed them and knew not to wait for them as they never crossed. However, A. Barrett Jenkins had written that there was 'no truth' in such stories.

In 1958 **Miss R I Clarke** of Norwich wrote to the *East Anglian Magazine*, saying that she had talked to a woman who claimed she had seen the ghostly figures of a man and a boy who had drowned whilst crossing by ferry. The woman said it had happened two years previously when, looking up suddenly, she saw them waiting for the boat and wondered how they could have passed her without being noticed. As she looked, she saw that 'a veil seemed to descend and they disappeared.' She later heard about the Walberswick ghost on a radio programme, and was convinced that was who the mysterious passengers had been.

The radio programme had been broadcast by the BBC in December 1955, when the spectral man and boy were described, along with the ferryman's comment 'I never wait for them' – which Todd had apparently been saying some sixty years earlier!

After the programme, which had caused quite a stir, a reporter for the *Lowestoft Journal* set out to ask if anyone else had had similar experiences. He found that few people in Walberswick even seemed to know about the mystery, and so he asked ferryman Bob Cross. Old Bob, then aged 82, replied that he had been working on the ferry for 60 years and this was the first he'd heard of it 'If it had happened even before I was on the ferry I should have heard of it. My brother – he died a year ago – had been on the ferry as well and he never spoke of it.'

Asked about the possibility of spooky sightings in the winter months he replied, 'When I was young I used to go into Southwold and I've come back across the ferry all hours of the night, winter and summer. Never saw a thing.'

Other locals, including the vicar, were approached and answered in the negative, but many suggested the reporter talk to Herbert 'Scarborough' English, then aged 76. He too had heard the story on the 'wireless' but reckoned that it was his own father and his son who had been seen, as they often walked down to the ferry but didn't cross. The journalist went away none the wiser.

In more recent years David Church and Chris Coleman insisted that they had seen a man waiting for the ferry, but he vanished as they drew near to fetch him. David's wife Julie had been told as a child that if you weren't careful when you walked on the ferry jetty, a ghostly hand might reach up through the timbers and grab your ankle. A terrifying thought for a child!

Again, there are vague stories about a ghostly woman who waits for her child to come back on the ferry, but no-one knows who she is. And of course, the river bank is said to be part of the 'devil dog' Black Shuck's territory.

The river can spark all kinds of thoughts and visions, especially on misty days or in stormy weather. But almost always it is a place of peace and calm, of natural beauty and simple pleasure. A place to stop and while away time.

Ferry-woman
A Poem by Paul Thompson

An old profession, perhaps
The oldest; where fords gave way
To bridges, which sank
In shifting sands, your hands
Grow rough on oars

On high days and holy-days
At high tide or low
Before life and after words
When dreaming dies
You row these shores

The stillness of the afternoon
The explosion of the dawn
Sometimes in sleeping
No-one can be there
To be the ferryman

Then we must yearn
Or walk upstream
Where marshes burn
And skylarks gleam
But ever returns

Your ferry, reliable
As the tide; biding not
To heal your calluses
Ladylike and very real.

The Ferry Song
by Chris Coe, 2003

Chorus:
Hard, push hard, push away from the side
Row fast, row hard head against the tide
Then easy drift use the tide! Easy glide use the tide!
The ferry moves over the Blyth
Til we reach the other side

Verses:
1. I am their old river, their gate to the seaways
   I join up the peoples but keep them apart,
   Over the bridge, but quicker by ferry –
   Southwold and Walberswick's heart.
   > There's been a ferry nigh 800 years
   > And I've seen the ferrymen come and go.
   > Boats with chains and boats that are steamers,
   > Working, wooden boats that they row.

2. I'm "Oud Bob", the ferryboat – good old clinker,
   I work with my youngster – "Halcyon Days",
   The people come laughing, watching or crossing,
   Yarning with strangers and paying their ways.
   > "Oh no! It's a woman" the young men they whisper
   > "She'll drown us for sure, we'll be swept out to sea!"
   > Folk tell her the same jokes, ask the same questions,
   > Send cards from the kids, and she loves them like me.

3. I am the ferryman, proud of my working,
   Just like my family, my father before.
   Carrying passengers, dogs, bikes and elephants,
   Boxes and bags from the grocery store.
   > Early morning's my peace and quiet –
   > Mist on the river, the sun is still low.
   > No wind, no engine, just the cry of the seabirds
   > And the dip of my oars as I row.

Walberswick ferry Lyrics
from 'Singing the River'
by Bridget Cousins 2007

Row, row, Walberswick ferry
Heigh ho, as the merry river flows

For hundreds of years, here a ferry has carried us o'er
Safe to the shore.

Row, row, Walberswick ferry
Heigh ho, as the merry river flows

Now on the pier, see the families, babies and gear
Picnics and beer

Row, row, Walberswick ferry
Heigh ho, as the merry river flows

See how the tide pulls the ferryboat, strong arms and hands
Haul for the strand

Row, row, Walberswick ferry
Heigh ho, as the merry river flows
Safe on the shore, laughing passengers leaving the quay
Head for the sea

Row, row, Walberswick ferry
Heigh ho, as the merry river flows

Only the faces change… Above: *Walberswick men stop for a chat c1920s (l to r)*
Albert English, Tow Cooper, Wessy Cross, George English
Below: c1970s William Geen, Phillip Kett snr, Dinks Cooper, Dubber English

The End

(or is it?)

Ferry Kids

Dani's son Charlie and Polly's son Oscar – the next generation of Southwold – Walberswick ferrymen?

Bibliography

A Visit to Southwold by A Barrett Jenkins 1983

Diary of James Maggs 1797 – 1890 by James Maggs,
Alan Bottomley, Alan Farquhar Bottomley
Boydell Press 2007   ISBN 9781843833277

Southwold River by Rachel Lawrence
Suffolk Books 1990   ISBN 086055144X

Story of Southwold edited by Janet Becker
F Jenkins 1948

Suffolk Within Living Memory compiled by the Suffolk
Federation of Women's Institutes
Countryside Books 1994   ISBN 185306288X